Written Also for Our Sake

9.97
CBD

Written Also for Our Sake

Paul and the Art of Biblical Interpretation

James W. Aageson

Westminster/John Knox Press
Louisville, Kentucky

© 1993 James W. Aageson

Scripture quotations from the New Revised Standard Version of the Bible are copyright © 1989 by the Division of Christian Education of the National Council of the Churches of Christ in the U.S.A., and are used by permission.

Book design by Victoria Robinette

First edition # 2663484 7

Published by Westminster/John Knox Press
Louisville, Kentucky

PRINTED IN THE UNITED STATES OF AMERICA
9 8 7 6 5 4 3 2 1

Library of Congress Cataloging-in-Publication Data

Aageson, James W., 1947–
    Written also for our sake : Paul and the art of biblical
interpretation / James W. Aageson. — 1st ed.
        p.   cm.
    Includes bibliographical references and index.
    ISBN 0-664-25361-X (pbk. : alk. paper)

    1. Bible. N.T. Epistles of Paul—Relation to the Old Testament.
2. Bible. O.T.—Hermeneutics.   3. Bible. O.T.—Quotations in the
New Testament.   I. Title.
BS2655.R32A33   1993
227'.06—dc20
                                                    92-33996

Contents

For My Parents
from whom much has been received

Acknowledgments

Without the stimulation and critique of colleagues, this book would not have been written. To my colleagues in the religion department at Concordia College in Moorhead, Minnesota, especially Larry Alderink and James Haney, a special word of thanks is due. Their friendship and critical comments have guided me and have clearly made this a better book. Special words of appreciation also go to Terry Fretheim of Luther Northwestern Theological Seminary, who read the manuscript and responded with helpful and insightful comments. Thanks as well to Jeff Hamilton of Westminster/John Knox Press, whose steady editorial hand and helpful suggestions proved invaluable. And most especially to my wife, Julie, and my daughters, Erin, Anne, and Megan, thanks for your encouragement and constant support.

Prologue

As a student of the Bible, I am interested, of course, in the way biblical texts are used, interpreted, and taught. Moreover, I have often found studies devoted to theoretical hermeneutics inadequate because they do not give sufficient attention to the character of the biblical texts themselves. Hence, I have devised this project as a study in biblical interpretation from the point of view of a theory applied directly to the texts of Paul's epistles. Following a brief sketch of what can be described as a "conversation model" of hermeneutics, I have sought to frame a way of understanding Paul's use and interpretation of scripture (the Old Testament). The assumption informing the organization of this book is that a model of hermeneutics should correspond clearly and directly to the way an interpreter actually uses a series of biblical texts. This, of course, requires careful attention to texts, in this case Pauline texts. This approach has a twofold advantage: (1) It raises issues of general, methodological importance to the field of biblical interpretation, and (2) it draws the reader directly into the substance of Paul's epistles.

The "conversation model" of hermeneutics is not, narrowly speaking, a literary-critical or a historical-critical model. Rather, it is a theoretical perspective that seeks to account for both approaches to the study of the Bible. In sketching this model of interpretation, I have sought to describe not only what I think takes place in the interpretation of scripture but also, for modern interpreters, how I think the task ought to be conceived and approached. This model then becomes the methodological point of reference for the ensuing examination of Paul's interpretation of scripture. This approach means that those instances in which Paul explicitly and self-consciously turns to the interpretation of scripture are of most immediate concern. The many echoes or allusions to scripture found in Paul's letters are only of indirect relevance for this study.

Many detailed studies of Paul's use of scripture have been written in English, German, and French. Most recently Richard Hays has written a fine literary-critical study of intertextuality in Paul entitled *Echoes of Scripture in the Letters of Paul*.[1] Others have examined the technical Jewish character of Paul's use of the Old Testament,[2] as well as the theological implications of his reliance on scripture.[3] In one way or another, virtually all of these studies have a bearing on this book. In contrast to them, however, I have sought to view Paul in the context of a more general theory of hermeneutics, a theory that also pertains to the way modern readers may in fact engage biblical texts. It is hoped that the outcome of this approach might shed light on Paul's use of scripture, as well as stimulate thinking about the interpretation of biblical texts. If these goals are accomplished, it will be evident that communities of faith, and also communities of scholars, who use and rely on biblical texts are engaged in an ongoing process of interpretation in which new conversations with scripture are constantly unfolding. Thus, biblical interpretation is and ought to be an open-ended process.

This book is written primarily for nonspecialists who are interested in the interpretation of biblical texts, especially Pauline texts. Students, pastors, and teachers are encouraged to use this book to generate their own thinking about Paul and the interpretation of the Bible. It will become clear to the reader that the concern of this book is not simply the theology of Paul but rather the process of forming a conceptual framework and developing a religious posture. Hermeneutics is one part of that process. This concern requires the reader to look beyond Paul's theological and religious conclusions to the ferment within his writing and his use of scripture. In Paul, we see a theology in the process of formation rather than a developed systematic theology expressed in epistolary form. This in itself makes Paul's letters an exciting focus for our investigation. In a rapidly changing world filled with unprecedented challenges, it may well be that modern communities are thrust into a similar situation of having to form and reform their own systems of belief. If that is the case, understanding the process of reformulation is as important as knowing the theologies and dogmas that have already been formulated. In that regard, Paul can be a worthy mentor once again, for he shows us the tensions and possibilities inherent in moving beyond accepted theological and religious frontiers.

Conversation
and Scripture

I

Ancient Text, Modern Book:
Toward a Theory of Interpretation

For the interpreter of the Bible, there is a tension between the Bible as a modern book and the Bible as an ancient set of texts. That which was written long ago is claimed to have validity for the present. But how and in what sense is it valid for the present? What is the relationship between those texts produced centuries ago and the book so cleverly bound and mass produced that is set before the interpreter today? Our difficulty as interpreters of the Bible is not unlike the dilemma that confronted Paul. His sacred, and in many cases ancient, texts were being put in the service of a contemporary religious community, a community separated from the origin of those very texts by time, theological outlook, and religious circumstance. The divide between the twentieth century and the world of the Bible is certainly more dramatic than between Paul and the world of his Bible. But the fact that there is a divide between the ancient texts and the sacred book to which later interpreters turn is unavoidable. The bridging of that divide between the biblical text and the interpreter's modern context is at the very heart of the interpretation of the Bible.

The interpreter of sacred texts always approaches the material as an outsider. The Bible is composed of a set of texts from a world that is foreign to us, and when we encounter its pages we enter into this strange and unfamiliar world. Indeed, the biblical world is often puzzling and confusing to modern readers. It often defies our view of reality and presents us with images and symbols that challenge our sense of how the world works. Perceptive biblical interpreters will invariably be impressed by the remoteness of the Bible and the sociohistorical categories within which its messages are contained. For many this leads to the conclusion that the Bible is basically irrelevant or has little to contribute to the modern world. To be sure, this conclusion says as much about the person who draws it as it does about the Bible itself. That this is the case, however, supports the contention that the value and the meaning of the Bible are determined by the relationship between the text and the interpreter. When the chasm between the two is so great that no meaningful encounter is finally possible, then understanding itself is not possible. The Bible has effectively ceased to be a living text and comes to be seen as a relic of the past. At most, it may be viewed by some as being of antiquarian interest. But for the edification of the human spirit, the education of the human mind, the remembering of the past, and the shaping of contemporary religious questions, the Bible has ceased for all effective purposes to function.

Yet, for many people, the situation is quite the reverse. Rather than being impressed by the great divide that separates text and interpreter, many fail to realize or choose to ignore the separation altogether. The historical integrity of the text is collapsed into what the interpreter determines the text's contemporary relevance to be. The distinction between interpreter and text is blurred if not lost entirely (this seems to be the case in some "newer" forms of literary criticism and perhaps also in certain theological readings of the Bible). In the most extreme form of this use of the Bible, the meaning of the text is simply what it means to the interpreter. The biblical text has no independent substance or reality. The meaning of the material is fashioned into a kind of reflection of the interpreter's own ideology. A sense of historical perspective on the text is lost. The interpreter's sense of the present overwhelms the historical, literary, and rhetorical integrity of the biblical text.

As I will propose in the following chapters, Paul has used his biblical text within the general parameters of what I have chosen to call a conversation model of interpretation. This is not to suggest that Paul actually thought in these terms, and it is clear that he was unaware of many constraints and considerations that modern interpreters must, in my judgment, take into account. Nevertheless, I will seek to illustrate that the conversation model gives us a framework for understanding and evaluating Paul's encounter with his biblical texts. Furthermore, I shall argue in this opening chapter that, with certain constraints, the conversation model is an appropriate way for modern readers of the Bible to conceive of their task as interpreters. Let there be no mistake: This does not mean that modern biblical hermeneutics can or should try to repristinate Pauline methodology. Our context is different. Our sense of appropriate and acceptable interpretation is different. The state of our knowledge and our traditions of interpretation are not those of Paul's day. Moreover, our modern views of the world are in many ways peculiar to our own circumstance in time and place. But the proposal to be set forth here allows for these differences and still gives us, as modern interpreters, a way of understanding what in fact takes place when we read, exegete, and explicate biblical texts. It can provide parameters for understanding and evaluating the process of biblical hermeneutics. It can provide a framework for realizing the pitfalls and dangers inherent in seeking to make sense of historical texts. And if this proposal is sound, it will describe generally what interpreters in fact are doing when they interpret biblical texts, whether they are aware of it or not. In this chapter, I am sketching a hermeneutical theory rather than proposing a set of interpretive techniques.

Toward a Theory of Interpretation

At the heart of the hermeneutical problem, as I see it, is the relationship between the biblical text and its context. This involves both the original context of the biblical documents and the context of the contemporary interpreter, the one who in any age comes to the task of discerning the meaning of the Bible. The biblical texts are grounded historically and socially in a set of circumstances, and they are shaped and conditioned by those circumstances. The ancient texts did not emerge in a historical or literary vacuum. They are very human kinds of products that display all the characteristics of human literary productions. Thus, if there is to be any control in the process of biblical interpretation, the complexity of these circumstances and the ways they have molded the biblical texts ought to be studied, I would argue, with rigor. Moreover, these texts can be studied as any other form of literature in order that the interpreter might discover what it was from a social, historical, and religious point of view that breathed life into them in their ancient context. In short, the Bible as an ancient book has an ancient context, and modern interpreters ignore the serious study of that ancient context at the risk of imposing, with no self-awareness, their own ignorance or ideology on the text. It is in seeing ancient texts in relation to their ancient contexts that the possibilities of meaning often begin to emerge. What was it that motivated and directed the biblical writers? What was it that filled the biblical writers with passion and gave them a sense of urgency? What gave their writings the depth and texture that has allowed them to endure through the generations? With serious attention to the recon-struction of the circumstances that produced these ancient texts, the Bible begins to become comprehensible to modern minds, while at the same time retaining its historical character and literary integrity. By keeping the Bible's ancient context clearly in view, the Bible is prevented from becoming a theological abstraction devoid of time and place, devoid of human pathos.

But surely the issue of context is more complicated than has just been outlined. If it were simply a matter of reaching out and taking hold of the information related to the ancient context of the Bible, there would be no issue. But such is not the case. The ancient context is not always accessible to us. Often we do not have enough informa-tion available to us. And in many cases we do not know how to assess the information we do have available to us. To greater or lesser degrees the Bible is shrouded in historical obscurity. This is certainly not to say that we can know little or nothing about the ancient biblical context. That is not the case. It is, however, to acknowledge the limitations of what we can know from a historical point of view about the biblical context.

Still, the problem is not really a matter of a lack of information. Rather, it is that the people who approach the biblical text, the interpreters, occupy their own contexts replete with their own views of what constitutes reality, knowledge, and truth. Since the worldview of biblical interpreters is almost always not the worldview of the biblical text, there is a tendency for unsuspecting interpreters to peer into the scriptural text and see little more than a mirror reflection of themselves and their own context. In that case, the biblical text has been unwittingly extracted from its historical context. It has become what the biblical interpreter wants it to become. This problem, however, does not simply present a dilemma for the untrained. It is a problem that in fact confronts every interpreter of biblical material. It is not the prerogative of interpreters of historical and literary texts to shed their contexts as so much excess baggage. That is not an option. Interpreters invariably bring to the task of explication their own questions, concerns, and understandings of reality. Interpreters without fail use the lens of their own context to bring into some kind of focus the texts that are to be interpreted. This situation is unavoidable because interpreters always approach the text from their own perspective and seek to communicate their view of the text to an audience of their own choosing. That is what Paul did, and that is what we do.

Therefore, biblical hermeneutics is carried out between the twin poles of biblical context on the one hand and interpretive context on the other. To ignore the context of the biblical texts is to lose the integrity of the text. It is to make the Bible over into our own image, which in Judeo-Christian terms would be a rather ironic form of idolatry. To ignore the context of the interpreter is to lose sight of the creative human contribution to the art of textual understanding. It is in its own way a denial of the common humanity of the text and the interpreter and of the human character of the interpretive process. To collapse these two poles, or to emphasize one to the detriment of the other, is to impede, if not make impossible, serious interpretive conversation. In my view, the integrity of both the biblical text and the interpreter must be maintained for a serious and vital interpretive dialogue to take place. Unlike a monologue, a dialogue requires a conversation partner. It involves engagement and encounter with the "other." It involves listening as well as speaking.[1]

What then does this suggest about the way we are to proceed with the art of biblical interpretation? We ought at the outset to disabuse ourselves of the notion that biblical texts contain a single meaning and that exegesis is analogous to trying to find the proverbial needle in the haystack. Biblical texts do not simply contain meaning but perhaps even more importantly they contribute to the generation and formation of meaning. They open up possibilities for meaning to be constructed and communicated. If this is true, biblical interpretation as a theological enterprise is more than simply trying to find God's will hidden among the literary clutter of the Bible. It is a matter of encountering the biblical text in order to mold and remold a worldview, within which divine address and human obedience are made possible. Biblical interpretation as an academic enterprise is a matter of generating a literary, historical, and sociological perspective that communicates something about the nature of the text's world, the text's character, and the text's significance. But in both cases, the process is carried out in terms that have the possibility of being intelligible to and understood by the interpreter's modern audience. Contemporary thought forms and language are the material out of which interpretive conclusions are formed and generated.

Hence, the process of biblical interpretation should not be envisioned as a mining enterprise in which the interpreter bores a shaft into the text in order to extract from the text its abundance of wealth. Rather, it should be understood as an interaction, similar to a dialogue, between text and interpreter. Without the text there is no interpretation. Without the interpreter the text remains mute and lifeless. This interaction can, of course, be conducted on many different levels. It can be undertaken with great skill and sophistication by those highly trained in historical, linguistic, and literary analysis. But it may also be entered into by those with relatively little sophistication in these matters. To say that the Bible is a closed book to all but a few highly trained people is patently untrue. Interaction between text and interpreter does not presuppose a high level of skill on the part of the interpreter, as desirable as that certainly is. It does, however, depend on a willing interpretive partner.

According to this way of viewing the interpretive process, exegetical technique will function to structure the conversation between the interpreter and the biblical text. For example, distinctions between what the text "meant" and what the text "means" and between "explanation," "understanding," and "interpretation" may have value in structuring a disciplined dialogue between the interpreter and the text. They may also be useful in enabling the interpreter to interrogate the biblical text and in that way to discover the richness of the text. The development of critical historical and literary tools for the modern study of the Bible has been important for precisely this reason. These tools have enabled interpreters to speak as well as to listen to the texts in new and more disciplined ways.

But interpretive technique as such does not negate our conversation theory of interpretation. Indeed, one of the negative consequences of the development of modern critical approaches has often been the implicit assumption that these tools are value neutral and that they lead the interpreter to results that are naively considered to be objective. Most astute interpreters of the Bible today realize this is not the case and are aware that critical methods are in many ways governed by the presuppositions of the Enlightenment, the university, the West, and males. In other words, they are as much a part of the interpreter's context as were the assumptions that guided the "fourfold" method of interpretation centuries before the advent of modern critical scholarship. From the first moment the biblical text is encountered, the interpreter's context comes into play, and the methods that are considered appropriate in that context serve to structure the way the interpretive conversation is to be undertaken. Exegetical tools do not allow the interpreter to escape the constraints of the conversation model of interpretation. On the contrary, I would argue that the study of interpretive methodology will itself finally lead to a recognition of some form of the conversation model of interpretation.

In light of what has been said to this point, one can legitimately ask whether this argument does not in effect mean that biblical interpretation is basically a matter of individual preference, choice, and insight. In other words, does the text mean whatever the individual interpreter wants it to mean? The short answer to this question is "By no means." Not, that is, if serious attention is given to the interactive nature of the dialogue between text and interpreter. The longer answer is that the text is a partner in the interpretive conversation. It places certain constraints on the interpreter. There are certain things that a biblical text cannot mean and that it cannot do. For if a scriptural text can mean anything, it will eventually come to mean everything and will in the end mean nothing. The biblical text does have its own integrity as a historical and literary document.

We may look at the issue in this way. To the extent that the text contains meaning as a historical or literary product, the task for the interpreter is to be drawn into what may be called a "circle of plausibility." By seeking to discover the meaning and significance of a particular biblical passage, we come to understand that there are some things the text does not mean and at the same time we come to realize that there are a number of plausible interpretations of the passage. It must be stated forthrightly at this point that the parameters of a "circle of plausibility" are neither absolute nor always very clear. These parameters are determined by communities, both religious and scholarly communities, and by the traditions that emerge from these communities. A "circle of plausibility" only begins to come into view when an interpretive consensus begins to form. The stronger the consensus, the more sharply defined are the parameters of the "circle of plausibility." As a community's consensus begins to break down, the lines become more blurred and unclear. A tradition of interpretation is to greater or lesser degrees simply an interpretive consensus that has formed and endured over a period of time. This is true in religious and in scholarly communities alike. It also means that there are different communities and traditions that will draw the parameters of acceptable biblical interpretation differently. And this suggests that several "circles of plausibility" may be in view at any one time. It also suggests that a single individual may operate in more than one "circle of plausibility." For example, a person may be a practicing member of a particular Christian tradition with its own parameters of accepted biblical interpretation, while at the same time be an active participant in a guild of scholars that operates with a quite different set of parameters.

The most immediate way to judge whether or not a set of interpretive conclusions fits within a "circle of plausibility" is to determine how these conclusions square with the accepted conclusions of a tradition of interpretation or some other kind of interpretive

consensus. The emphasis is on "orthodox" interpretation. This applies
to both religious and scholarly traditions. In many cases the two are all
but indistinguishable. But in both, the criterion for determining the
"circle of plausibility" is the tradition accepted as normative by the
given community. According to the standard of first-century Jewish
interpretation, many if not all of Paul's interpretive conclusions were
considered outside the "circle of plausibility." Likewise, according to
the standards of the sixteenth century, many of the biblical interpretations of the Protestant reformers were considered outside the parameters of accepted biblical understanding. And to be sure, Karl Barth's
publication of *The Epistle to the Romans* in 1918 did not meet with the
overwhelming approval of biblical scholars educated in the traditions
of nineteenth-century Europe. Judging the adequacy of biblical
interpretation according to standards of "orthodoxy," if applied
rigorously, will mean the preservation of the hermeneutical status quo.
This method of defining the "circle of plausibility" has its place, but it
is certainly not the only way, and probably not even the best way, of
doing so.

From the opposite direction, biblical interpretations may be judged
not against the standard of "orthodoxy," but retrospectively by the
degree to which they precipitate and indeed establish their own
consensus or "circle of plausibility." In other words, what has been the
effect of a particular way of looking at biblical texts? Has a particular
view come to function with sufficient persuasiveness and power that it
spawns its own tradition of biblical interpretation? In this case, the
parameters of biblical interpretation are drawn only in retrospect.
They are drawn as a community finds within a particular interpretive
perspective something that persuades it of the truthfulness of that
perspective and compels it to continue the work that has been done.
This is the material of which traditions are made. This is also the
material out of which new methods are developed and new insights
multiplied. It is also a process that challenges older traditions and calls
into question the validity of "orthodox" solutions to hermeneutical
problems. In this light, Paul's christological use of the Bible certainly
receives a more favorable judgment. And that is true of all biblical
interpreters who have moved beyond the bounds of "orthodoxy" to

discover unexplored territory. These people have often become figures of controversy, but in the end their work could not be ignored by the defenders of the hermeneutical status quo because in them and in their work new and enticing visions of reality have begun to capture the religious and intellectual imaginations of people. Because of the work of Paul and other such innovators, the interpretive landscape would never again be the same.

This is not to suggest that religious and scholarly "orthodoxies" are simply overturned by the power of hermeneutics. It often seems to be the case that the demise of an "orthodoxy" is in significant measure the result of changed historical, intellectual, and religious circumstances, which render that "orthodoxy" implausible or at least no longer able to address the pressing concerns and questions of people. In this case, new interpretive perspectives and insights on the Bible are part of a larger readjustment of the "circle of plausibility." Thus, a new hermeneutical perspective can be born of changed intellectual circumstances and at the same time contribute to the formation of a new religious worldview.

A corollary to this second way of defining the parameters of biblical interpretation is to look at the human and historic consequences of a particular hermeneutical outlook. For example, the controversies between Jesus and the Jewish authorities in the Gospels have historically been interpreted as a condemnation of the legalism and sterile religion of the Jews. Moreover, the Jews have been labeled hermeneutically as "Christ killers." Only recently have these interpretive assumptions been challenged and shown to be morally offensive. But one consequence of these conclusions or assumptions has been to permit, justify, and indeed encourage various kinds of horror perpetrated by Christians against Jews down through the centuries. Against this backdrop of pogrom and persecution, Christian interpreters of the tradition have been called upon to reevaluate their hermeneutical "circle of plausibility." This does not mean that interpreters are to engage in a whitewashing of the tradition, but it does mean that they are to come to the sacred texts fully aware of the way traditions of interpretation have been used and of the way their own interpretations might be used. In short, perceptive interpreters of the Bible consciously bring to their task an awareness of the forces that have shaped their own context.

In the process of identifying the "circle of plausibility," it is desirable to think of both the biblical text and the interpreter as "subjects" in a joint conversation. For an interactive dialogue to be possible, there must be a mutually informing encounter between an identifiable text and an autonomous interpreter. The interpreter, in fact, addresses and questions the biblical text. In turn, the biblical text responds and confronts the interpreter who listens and discerns the meaning of what is being said. The process is interactive and dynamic. At its best, it is a dialogical encounter in which both partners speak and both partners listen and in which neither can be said to possess or fully understand the other. To be sure, there are often lopsided conversations. One partner does most of the speaking, while the other does most of the listening. Yet, a good conversation involves give and take between two partners who actively engage one another.

This is clearly a metaphorical way of understanding the character of biblical hermeneutics, but it has the clear advantage of not allowing the biblical text to be reduced to an inert object that is simply acted upon or manipulated by the interpreter. On the contrary, the biblical text has its own contribution to make to the dialogue. The biblical text provides the interpreter with a vocabulary for continuing the conversation or for understanding the interpreter's own context. Thus, the biblical text is as much a "subject" engaged in the dialogue as is the interpreter. When the biblical interpreter, mistakenly in my view, sees the text of the Bible as an inanimate object or as merely a specimen to be analyzed, the interpreter quite naturally diminishes the "subjectivity" (life) of the text. Moreover, this can result in the deception that ultimate mastery over the text as an object has been achieved by the interpreter. Whenever historical and literary criticism have resulted in the thoroughgoing "objectification" of the biblical text, they have, I suggest, refused to engage the biblical text as a conversation partner. The text has been relegated to an object of analysis.

To think of the biblical text hermeneutically as a "subject" engaged in a conversation can have important implications for the process of biblical interpretation. First, this concept helps prevent one from predetermining the conclusions to be drawn from the text. The interpreter cannot presume to know what the text means before the text has had a chance to speak. Second, it encourages the interpreter to listen seriously to the text and to observe carefully its character. It can instill respect for the biblical text. Third, the notion of conversation requires that the interpreter come to understand clearly that the text and the interpreter are not identical. The concerns and questions of the biblical interpreter are not necessarily the concerns and questions of the biblical text. It prevents the divide between the interpreter and the text from being ignored. Fourth, it has the potential to prevent the art of biblical interpretation from slipping into absolute relativism in which there is no control over what is good or bad interpretation. The boundaries between the plausible and the implausible are acknowledged and sought by the interpreter who respects the substance and "subjectivity" of the text. Fifth, the idea of conversation as applied to the text of the Bible can force the interpreter to modify previously held positions. It can stimulate an openness that undermines and subverts old ways of looking at the material. It can stimulate fresh possibilities of meaning. Finally, the concept of hermeneutical conversation can provide a basis for conversation between interpreters who operate in different "circles of plausibility." Conversations with biblical texts should also stimulate conversations between biblical interpreters.

In light of what has been said to this point, it should be evident that biblical hermeneutics will invariably give rise to interpretive pluralism. It is inevitable that there will be debates and differences of viewpoint by those who take biblical interpretation seriously. There is, of course, a great deal of bad biblical interpretation around, but the debates in our society over the use and understanding of the Bible are not new. In one form or another, they have been going on since scripture was first determined to be scripture. The Pharisees and Sadducees of the first century probably had debates over the relation between scripture and tradition. The sixteenth century also saw debates over the authority of scripture and tradition. Hence, informed people need not be surprised that such controversies take place today.

While this interpretive pluralism is inevitable, it testifies in its own way to the richness of the biblical texts and to the inherent diversity of the Bible. The Bible is itself the product of religious and interpretive pluralism. The New Testament did not emerge out of a homogeneous religious community. And the early Christian community does not represent a "golden age" of the church that the modern community should try to recreate. Quite the opposite: the church of the New Testament period displayed considerable diversity and even schism. Neither was the New Testament church of one theological mind. There was great theological diversity in the early period of the church. A study of Paul's letters vividly illustrates this.

Scholarly and religious interpretation of sacred texts will continue as long as people are attracted to the biblical texts. By its very nature, interpretation of the Bible is an unfinished enterprise. The conversation between the ancient texts and the interpreter's context is always shifting. It is always in a state of change. There are always new ways of construing the meaning of biblical material and new ways of understanding the world that produced the texts of the Bible. Moreover, serious-minded men and women who wish to deal with the Bible have the responsibility to be good conversation partners in the interpretive dialogue. The more interesting the interpreter, the more interesting the Bible will be. Just as a good conversation with someone takes work and skill, so does good biblical interpretation. To see the richness of the biblical texts requires a degree of self-consciousness and self-awareness on the part of the interpreter. At its best, hermeneutics involves knowledge of appropriate methods of interpretation, and it encourages understanding of the ways these methods can be applied, in order that the sacred texts can speak. Regardless of one's level of training, however, biblical interpretation requires more than sincerity. It demands disciplined dialogue. It also demands a willingness to be a part of the ongoing corporate enterprise of biblical hermeneutics. In this corporate dialogue with the text and with one's fellow interpreters, the threat of hermeneutical anarchy subsides and the development of new traditions of interpretation is made possible.

Implicit throughout this discussion has been the conviction that the Bible is not finally a sectarian set of documents. It is a public book, and that means that it will be read by different people from a variety of different contexts. The Bible is a book of the academic community just

as it is a book of believing communities, churches and synagogues. The
Bible can be used to train the minds of the young just as it can be used
to edify the faith of the old. An appreciation of the biblical interpretation of others will require first an understanding of the context and the
purpose of the interpreter. A refusal to examine these will lead
eventually to bigotry and provincialism, the very things that both
religion and scholarship ought to resist. Where fundamental differences do exist in the ways the Bible is understood and used, the issues
must be examined according to critical and rational considerations and
not sectarian passions. In the interaction between the text of the Bible
and the context of the interpreter, the richness of these ancient texts
can be discovered, and the enduring value of this modern book can be
encountered once again.

Conclusion

Paul's use of the Bible cannot be judged by the standards established
for modern interpretive methodology. Neither can modern interpreters be expected to conform to Paul's use of biblical texts. In both cases,
this would be a hermeneutical anachronism. Moreover, it would be an
implicit denial of the conversation model of interpretation. Paul
worked with his biblical texts, and he interpreted them from the
perspective of his christological context. The skills of interpretation he
had learned as a Jew were placed in the service of a christological and
ecclesiological message, and the process of encountering his biblical
texts christologically propelled him into new religious and theological
territory. For Paul, the scriptural text had integrity, but it was also
capable of generating a message for his own time and situation.
Regardless of the way we react today to Paul's use of the Bible (Old
Testament), we too interact with our biblical text. We listen to it, and
we speak to it. Out of these encounters emerge the claims that we,
modern interpreters of scripture, wish to make about the intention,
meaning, and significance of the Bible (Old Testament and New
Testament). And perhaps we too will one day produce a vision of
biblical material that will capture the imagination of the human heart,
spirit, and mind.

The study of interpretation can be undertaken in many different ways. It can be investigated as a matter of theory by philosophers. It can also be understood conceptually as a function of literature. But I have chosen, following this theoretical sketch, to engage in interpretation for the express purpose of learning how a particular interpreter of scripture, namely Paul, goes about the business of hermeneutics. The approach here is somewhat analogous to learning an art form by studying the work of an ancient artist. Since we cannot speak directly to the artist, we must ourselves engage in an interpretive conversation with the legacy that the artist has left to us. In this case, it is the literary legacy of the apostle Paul.[2] Much as students of Michelangelo learn about the technique and skill of the master from studying his work, so, I propose, we can learn about the interpretive skill of the apostle from examining the way he does interpretation. But students of Michelangelo learn more than technique and approach. Through an encounter with the artist's painting and sculpture, students learn something about art itself and what is involved in the formation of art. We may not wish to consider Paul the consummate interpreter of scripture, but he is a worthy focus for our investigation because he has been so fundamentally important for the development of Christianity and Christian theology. Moreover, we can learn something about hermeneutics from him. In Paul's letters, we can see interpretation taking place in the context of a ministry to the Gentiles.

Two elements, however, must first be distinguished: theory and technique. In this chapter, I have sketched my theory of interpretation. I also think this theory exhibits a conceptual link with the way Paul encounters his biblical text and the images he draws from it. He, too, converses with biblical texts and reflects biblical imagery. But Paul's techniques are from his own age and religious circumstance as a Jew. They are not necessarily our techniques. By studying them, however, we can learn something about the way Paul constructs an argument and forms his theology. Even though these methods and techniques may not be our own, they are instructive for understanding the apostle and his letters. They give us a glimpse into the world of Paul and his literary legacy.

In chapters II and III of this book, I will examine the parameters of

Paul's conversation with scripture. I will also consider some of the
apostle's methods of using scripture in writing epistles to the emerging
Gentile churches. Throughout, there will be an effort to discover how
Paul might contribute to reflection in our own modern context within
the community of faith. In chapters IV through VII, I will focus
specifically on the way my interpretive theory and Paul's exegesis come
together in the formation of selected theological themes and ideas.
Once again, there will be an effort to see how these Pauline theological
claims are formative and important for our modern hermeneutical
context.

II

A Hebrew Born of Hebrews:
The Voice of Paul

Paul the Jew

Much as any modern interpreter of scripture, Paul encounters two worlds: the world of the biblical text and the world of his own context, first-century missionary work among the Gentiles. He is a Jew and an apostle of Christ to the Gentiles. These facts of Paul's life orient us with respect to the world in which he operates and which he seeks to address. He has heard the traditions of his people (Gal. 1:14; Phil. 3:4–6), and he has studied the Jewish scriptures. He is part of the world of first-century Hellenistic Judaism. But Paul is also a man possessed of the conviction that Christ crucified and risen is Lord and that he is to take the message of Christ to the Gentiles. Paul engages the world and he uses scripture to address it. As any serious expositor and preacher, he brings the word of scripture and the experience of his world into a mutually informing encounter.

Pauline scholars have often addressed the question: "What kind of Jew was Paul?" This question arises initially because a neat division between Paul's Greek and Jewish worlds is artificial. As a Jew of the dispersion, Paul lived in a world profoundly affected by Greek culture and Greek ways. There is no neat division between that which is Jewish and that which is Greek in Paul's world, for he lived in a world that was marked by acculturation and assimilation. Paul and the Judaism that he knew were shaped both by the culture of the Greeks and by the scriptures and traditions of Israel. Hence, it is often difficult to untangle the cultural and religious peculiarities of Hellenistic Judaism so that a sharp dividing line between discrete cultural and religious phenomena can be identified. For Jews and Christians living in America today, it is difficult to separate clearly religious and intellectual traditions from the common social and cultural milieu of North American life. So with Paul, the cultural and religious contexts are closely interconnected.

Yet the problem of understanding Paul is more involved than discerning the cultural complexities of the Hellenistic world. Paul's relationship to Judaism and the character of his religion have been issues of considerable debate among those who have studied Paul seriously. Pauline theology has been related to Judaism in various ways by scholars. It has been viewed as essentially antithetical to Judaism, though dependent on it for certain themes or motifs.[1] Others have understood Paul's seemingly negative attitude toward Judaism to be directed not against Palestinian Judaism but an inferior Hellenistic form of Judaism.[2] Some have argued that significant Pauline motifs are reflected in rabbinic literature and derive ultimately from Palestinian Judaism.[3] Paul's theology is thus not antithetical to Judaism but is grounded in the conviction that Jesus is the Messiah. Still others have viewed Paul in terms of Jewish eschatology or apocalypticism.[4] E. P. Sanders has declared that the pattern of Paul's religion can in fact be characterized as "participationist eschatology."[5]

The common element in these studies is a concern for the relationship of Pauline theology to some form of Judaism. This relationship provides interpreters of Paul with a vexing interpretive problem. Against what background is his theology to be understood? What is the religious impulse that drives his theology? What are the circumstances with which Paul must deal, and how does he respond to them? Even as modern expositors of Paul are compelled to understand something of their own world, they are also obliged to have an understanding of Paul's world. Krister Stendahl and, more recently, E. P. Sanders have shown that failure to attend to these issues can lead to a distortion of Paul's theology and its character, at least in exegetical terms.[6] Moreover, the Pauline text ends up being obscured behind the many theological presuppositions imposed upon it. Instead of the Pauline text itself being the primary conversation partner, the way the text has traditionally come to be understood becomes the starting point for further dialogue. In other words, the issue of Paul's Judaism and his Jewish context has important implications for the way his epistles are interpreted and his theology is used today.

The fact that Paul is a Jew requires that we consider his Jewish context—his Jewish voice—and the way it affects his conversation with scripture. Moreover, Paul's Christology itself is to be seen in connection with Judaism. In the theology of Paul, the two are interwoven. Indeed, Paul's apostolic context and his sense of being commissioned to proclaim the name of Christ to the Gentiles is to be viewed in the larger context of his allegiance to the covenant of Israel. In Paul's theology, apostolicity and being Jewish are not to be construed as fundamentally opposed or mutually antagonistic to one another. To be sure, the attempt to hold these together causes Paul some religious and theological difficulty. But this difficulty itself, which we will observe at many points in our discussion, testifies to the breadth of Paul's religious commitment. He will not—indeed cannot—abandon Israel and its God. He cannot forsake his conviction that the God of Israel has acted to bring salvation to the nations in Jesus Christ. Thus, he is compelled to reshape his religious worldview and the moral order that undergirds it. He is forced to reinterpret the character of God's covenant with Israel. Or, as Paul might say, he has been given to understand the essential meaning of the covenant, which has been hidden from all eternity. In Pauline theology, we get a glimpse of the religious metamorphosis that has been brought about by the apostle's attempt to rationalize and reconcile fundamental commitments. Among them are the belief that Jesus is the Son of the Jewish God, that the law is good and holy, that the people of Israel have not been abandoned by God, and that salvation is now universally available to all people. In one form or another, these commitments are inherent in Paul's apostolicity, his Christology, and his own sense of being a Jew.

Theology and Christology

Closely related to the issue of Paul's character as a Jew and to his conversation with the Jewish sacred texts is the relationship between theology and Christology. By theology I mean Paul's thinking about God, specifically the God of the Jews, and by Christology I mean the way Paul understands Christ to have become God's agent in the working out of redemption. It is clearly a mistake to characterize Paul's thought as somehow pitting theology and Christology against each other. Paul was and remained a monotheist. On three occasions in his epistles, Paul makes reference to the opening assertion of the *shema*, "Hear O Israel, the Lord our God is *one* . . ." (Rom. 3:30; Gal. 3:20; 1 Cor. 8:4). For Paul, God is one, and this one God is the God of Israel. The activity of God is recounted in the scriptures of Israel and is testified to by the prophets of old. Indeed, for Paul, the story of redemption itself is implicitly tied together by God and the activity of God. The apostle does not develop a theology based on the great acts of God throughout history (salvation-history), but he does presuppose underlying connections between what God has done in the past and what God is doing in the present.

The fact that Paul turns to scripture at all indicates that there are for him theological connections between that which is encountered or heard in the text of the Bible and the religious circumstances that he is facing in the present. For example, at the conclusion of the scriptural argument in Romans 4, Paul says: "Now the words, 'it was reckoned to him,' were written not for his sake alone, but for ours also" (Rom. 4:23–24). That which is true for Abraham is explicitly being affirmed as true for the present as well. The only way Paul can make this connection is if he accepts a theological link between the present and the past. The God who reckoned Abraham to be righteous in scripture is, for Paul, the same God who reckons the faithful to be righteous in his own day. Paul does not survey theologically the great redemptive acts of God in his epistles. Rather, he develops lines of correspondence between that which is true in scripture and that which is true in the present in light of Christ.[7] Paul's conviction that the God of the Jews has acted in Jesus Christ provides the conceptual structure for his encounter with scripture. Without this underlying framework, the apostle's conversation with the Bible would make little or no sense.

Paul's theological outlook, however, is also connected to his eschatological view of the world. Indeed, Paul's theology, as it is formed in relation to Judaism, is eschatological. Paul sees himself as living in the end time. He writes in 1 Corinthians 10:11: "These things happened to them to serve as an example, and they were written down to instruct us, on whom the ends of the ages have come." In the present age, God has acted to bring about the redemption of all the world, and this redemption is about to be finalized at the return of Christ. For Paul, the end of the age has come—"See, now is the acceptable time; see, now is the day of salvation!" (2 Cor. 6:2)—but the resurrection of the dead and the consummation of salvation is yet to be fulfilled (1 Cor. 15:51–54). The religious background for this concept is clearly Jewish apocalypticism (the words "apocalypse," "apocalyptic," and "apocalypticism" derive from the Greek term *apokalypsis,* which means "revelation").[8] Paul's theology, his understanding of the activity of God, has been shaped by the categories of Jewish apocalyptic thought. At a particular time, in the near future, the Jewish apocalyptist saw God preparing to act decisively. For Paul, that decisive act has now been set in motion in the events associated with Christ's death and resurrection.

The Jewish apocalyptic vision, however, had to be modified by the early followers of Christ. They associated the intervention of God with Jesus of Nazareth; and since Jesus has now lived and died, it is theologically necessary to account for the uniqueness of Christ's mission on earth and at the same time to hold out the expectation of God's ultimate act of fulfillment at some point in the future. Thus, there is a necessary relationship between the present and the future in the eschatological vision of the early disciples of Jesus. As they gathered following the events of Jesus' crucifixion and the experiences of Easter, the disciples began the arduous theological task of making sense of an apocalyptic vision of redemption, while at the same time bringing that vision into accord with the conviction that Jesus is the Messiah, the agent of God in bringing about the salvation of the world. Between the appearance of Christ on earth and his return, the world was understood to live in a state of salvation at once realized and at the same time yet to be fulfilled.

If Paul is still a Jew, even after assuming the mantle of apostleship, he must be viewed as an apocalyptic Jew. Other strands of Judaism also figure in Paul's religious experience and practice, but apocalypticism plays a prominent role in his concept of divine activity. It serves to structure the way he conceives of God's redemptive work in the world. It also undergirds his understanding of scripture. That which has been written in the past now applies to the present. That which has been testified to by the prophets has now come to pass in Christ. The purposes of God for the salvation of the world have been revealed in Jesus Christ.

Christology then is understood by Paul in terms of an overarching theological and apocalyptic world picture. Christ, identified as Jesus of Nazareth, is the agent of God in bringing about the new eschatological reality. Even more than the agent of God, Jesus is seen as the Son of God. In him the inauguration of the end times has come to pass. This is stated most pointedly in 2 Corinthians 5:17: "So if anyone is in Christ, there is a new creation: everything old has passed away; see, everything has become new!" The details of Paul's eschatology are beyond the purview of this discussion. Nevertheless, the terminology of this verse emphasizes the radical character of that which has been accomplished in the Christ-event, according to Paul. The language of old and new creation highlights in dramatic fashion the decisive quality of that which God has done in Jesus Christ. In the apocalyptic structure of reality, Christ is conceived as bringing the new age into the present. To be sure, Paul does not understand the old age to have finally passed away. But in the Christ-event, its ultimate end is heralded. Likewise, the new age in Christ is made a reality. It is to be consummated at the return of Christ.

If Paul is an apocalyptic Jew, he is also in some sense a messianic Jew. As we shall see, his messianism is peculiar when compared to popular conceptions of the messiah current in Judaism of his time.[9] Moreover, Paul's apocalyptic conceptions clearly work in tandem with his notions of the messiah. Not all apocalyptic Jews tied their apocalypticism to a messiah, but Paul and the other early followers of Jesus certainly did. Paul saw Christ as the messianic agent in the apocalyptic scheme of world events. To put it another way, Christ is the instrument of God in bringing about the apocalyptic vision of the new age. For Paul, theology shaped by an apocalyptic vision of reality is brought into harmony with the conviction that Jesus of Nazareth is the anointed one of God.

But this Jesus is a crucified Messiah (1 Cor. 15:3–8). Messiah is an English form of the Hebrew word *mashiah*, meaning "an anointed one." Anointing was an ancient Hebrew practice for commissioning a person to a divinely sanctioned office. Kings, prophets, and occasionally priests were appointed to their positions by the act of anointing.[10] In Greek, of course, the Hebrew word *mashiah* became *Christos*. As Alan Segal has noted, in the Greek world there was apparently no royal connotation to the term. In addition, it could even be associated with the athlete who anoints the body with oil before engaging in competition. Moreover, the Hebrew concept of *mashiah* pertains more to the idea of a divinely ordained function than it does a person.[11] In time, however, the term "messiah" came to be associated with the expectation that the messiah would sit upon the kingly throne of David. For the New Testament, as for the later rabbis, the messianic king was seen in connection with the promise to David in 2 Samuel 7.[12] In Judaism the prospect that the messiah would suffer is largely foreign to the tradition, though preliminary reports on some recently published Dead Sea scroll material suggest the concept may not be entirely unknown. Expressing the traditional scholarly view, Don Juel writes:

> No one expected the Messiah to suffer for sins. No one expected the Messiah to rise from the dead, because he was not expected to die. The biblical passages acknowledged as "messianic" in Jewish tradition are consistent in this regard.[13]

Hence, Paul's messianism is properly speaking the messianism represented by the early church. Jesus was a messianic figure who

suffered and died. Jewish biblical texts and conceptions contributed to
the early church's elaboration and transformation of its messianic
ideas. Paul was certainly influenced by these developing notions and
perhaps also contributed to them. Thus, Paul's messianism is clearly a
peculiar variety of messianism that emphasizes that Jesus carries out
his commission by suffering, dying, and rising. In fulfilling this
commission, he brings into the present the eschatological rule of God.

Theology and Christology are thus closely connected in the religious thought of Paul. They are developed in relation to apocalypticism and messianism, and they along with scripture provide the
material out of which the early Christian worldview emerged. This
connection between theology and Christology also makes unnecessary,
for Paul's understanding of scripture, a thoroughgoing theology of
salvation-history. Furthermore, Paul did not converse with scripture
from the perspective of a Christology that stands in complete opposition to Israel. Both a theological perspective that highlights continuity
and a Christology that emphasizes discontinuity between the past and
the present are operative in Paul. Both are formative in the development of his hermeneutic. To view Paul and his hermeneutic only in
terms of salvation-history is to lose sight of his christologically
informed dialogue with scripture. And to fail to see his Christology in
the context of a theologically informed apocalypticism is to lose hold of
the abiding importance of Israel and its scriptures for Paul.

Paul and the Law

As a Jew, Paul understands the centrality of the law for the covenant
between God and Israel. There is no reason to think that Paul had
become disenchanted with Judaism or that he chafed under the
requirements of a burdensome set of religious obligations.[14] To use E.
P. Sanders's terminology, Paul moved from "solution" to "plight" and
not from "plight" to "solution."[15] That is, he did not seek to escape
from Judaism because he found it defective or burdensome. Rather,
he came to a new understanding of Judaism retrospectively. If Jesus is
the Christ, the agent of God's redemption, he then becomes the key for
understanding Judaism. This is the intellectual move Paul made, and

it is this move that led ultimately to the apostle's redefinition of the Jewish law and its function. Paul the apostle did not sever his religious and theological connections with the law. As he states in Romans 7:12: "So the law is holy, and the commandment is holy and just and good." Yet Paul certainly came to understand the function of the law differently in light of Christ. To put it succinctly, the pride of place in Paul's religious system shifted from a divine-human relationship based upon Torah to a relationship established in Christ. Hence, Paul's religion is fundamentally messianic/eschatological rather than Torah-centered.

The problem of the law for Paul extends beyond the issue of theology. It is a problem that comes to bear on the way a person gets into the community of Christ and the way the unity of that community is preserved. In other words, the law poses a religious problem for the apostle to the Gentiles. On what basis does a Gentile become a member of the community of Christ? Is it through circumcision and adherence to the law of Moses? Or is it on some other basis? In this regard, the apostle is clear. Obedience to the law of Moses is not an entrance requirement into the community of Christ for Gentiles. Indeed, the law of Moses is not a universal requirement for the people of God in Christ. To impose this condition upon the Gentiles, according to Paul, is to resort to "works" rather than to rely on "grace."[16] In effect, Paul has transformed Judaism from a national religion into a universal religion through the incorporation of Gentiles into the community of Christ. Paul did not perceive this to be a negation of Judaism but a completion of Judaism and its task of being a blessing to the nations.

If the law of Moses is not universally binding either as an entrance requirement or as a condition of maintaining one's status in the community of Christ, for Paul, what is its value? If the law is of no value and never has been of any value, the justice of God is called into question. At the very least, God has been duplicitous. Thus, Paul is compelled, for the sake of the integrity of God, to assert that the law is good and holy. But if that is so, what is the purpose of the law in the face of Christ's coming? This is the question Paul is obligated by the logic of his own position to address. The law of Moses is a problem that has both religious and theological consequences for Paul: religious

consequences because the Gentile mission is at stake, and theological consequences because the integrity of God must be maintained.

In Galatians 3:19 Paul asks the pertinent question: "Why then the
law?" To which he answers: "It was added because of transgressions,
until the offspring would come to whom the promise had been
made."[17] Further on in the argument of Galatians, Paul writes in 3:24:
"Therefore the law was our disciplinarian until Christ came, so that we
might be justified by faith." This is followed in the beginning of
chapter 4 by the analogy of an heir who is placed under a guardian
until the appointed time when the full rights of inheritance shall be
made available. According to this explanation, the law's custodial
function is provisional. Implicit in this discussion is Paul's attempt to
give positive value and purpose to the law and at the same time to
preserve the uniqueness of Christ. He seeks to do this in three ways: (1)
by showing that the law is not contrary to the promises of God and
righteousness by faith, (2) by asserting that the law was given on
account of transgressions until Christ should come, and (3) by claiming
that the law has a tutorial function.

Paul's attempt to redefine the function of the law moves in a
different direction in Romans 7.[18] He writes in 7:7–8:

> What then should we say? That the law is sin? By no means! Yet, if it had
> not been for the law, I would not have known sin. I would not have
> known what it is to covet if the law had not said, "You shall not covet."
> . . . Apart from the law sin lies dead.

Similarly, in Romans 5:20 the apostle writes: "But law came in, with
the result that the trespass multiplied." Romans 7 is perhaps one of the
most complex texts in all of the Pauline epistles,[19] but it is clear from
this reference that Paul attributes to the law the awakening of sin.
Instead of the positive, albeit provisional, function ascribed to the law
in Galatians, the law in Romans serves a negative function. Indeed,
according to Romans 5:20, the law came in and increased the trespass of Adamic humanity. In any case, however, Paul strives to give
account of the law while at the same time making clear that he

does not accord to the law a saving function for the community of Christ.

To say that Paul's religion is not Torah-centered is not the same as saying that Paul is antilaw. Ethical assertions follow from the apostle's theological claims. For example, in Galatians 5:13–14 Paul states:

> For you were called to freedom, brothers and sisters; only do not use your freedom as an opportunity for self-indulgence, but through love become slaves to one another. For the whole law is summed up in a single commandment, "You shall love your neighbor as yourself."[20]

This statement follows the long and rather involved theological discussion of chapters 3 and 4 regarding faith and the law. Moreover, this exhortation from Galatians displays a connection between Paul's concern for moral laxity and the fulfillment of the law. To be sure, Paul was not the first to link obedience to the law and the love of one's neighbor. Rabbis did this as well. But Paul shows that the moral structure of the law continues to inform his sense of appropriate behavior in the community of Christ. It may very well be that the love of one's neighbor as the fruit of the Spirit (see Gal. 5:22–23) is the content of what Paul means by the term "law of Christ " (Gal. 6:2). In any case, it should be clear that Paul does not abandon all the moral underpinnings of the law. Still, he redefines the law and its function. He recenters his religion christologically, and he refuses to make obedience to the law an entrance requirement for the fellowship of Christ.

God's Covenant with the Jews

Paul is committed to the idea that God has made promises to Israel and that there is an abiding covenantal relationship. This conviction is not abandoned by Paul, the apostle of Christ. This covenantal bond between God and Israel is a tenet of Paul's emerging theology. "God has not rejected his people whom he foreknew" (Rom. 11:2). The appearance of Christ has not led to the abrogation of this covenant. On the contrary, the people of Israel still occupy an integral place in the unfolding of God's work of salvation. Speaking to the Gentiles in Romans 11:17–18, Paul writes:

> But if some of the branches were broken off, and you, a wild olive shoot, were grafted in their place to share the rich root of the olive tree, do not boast over the branches. If you do boast, remember that it is not you that support the root, but the root that supports you.

This, of course, is metaphorical language that maintains the theological primacy of Israel in the unfolding drama of salvation. It is a striking reaffirmation of Israel's abiding covenant with God. To be sure, Paul is troubled by the failure of most Jews to believe that Jesus is the Messiah. And it is certainly debatable whether or not the apostle understood the Jews as having a special track to salvation. Yet, Paul leaves little doubt that he expects Israel to partake in the salvation of God. "A hardening has come upon part of Israel, until the full number of the Gentiles has come in. And so all Israel will be saved" (Rom. 11:25–26). According to Paul, this is a mystery. It is nevertheless an assertion that indicates that the promises of God to the Jews still prevail, despite the "unbelief" of the vast majority of the people of Israel.

As we have seen, Paul's religious context is given its contour by Jewish messianism and apocalypticism. Moreover, we have argued that Paul's religious worldview is not centered in Torah but neither is it antilaw. To this is also added the concept of covenantalism. The promises of God are tied to a particular people. The working out of those promises for the world, according to Paul, has come to fruition in Jesus the Jew from Nazareth and in the carrying of his name to the nations. This christological conviction is not divorced in Paul's theology from a corresponding recognition that Jesus the Messiah is a representative of the covenant people. For Paul, he is the offspring promised to Abraham. Furthermore, he is the one through whom Israel has become a blessing to the nations. This covenant with Israel has become in Christ a covenant with the Gentiles, which, according to Paul, does not negate the promises made to Israel. However, in the universalization of the covenant concept, Paul has given impetus to a religious transmutation of historic Judaism. He has broadened the implication of the covenant, and he has severed this wider notion of covenant from strictly nationalistic boundaries.

Paul and Christ

In Galatians 1:15–16 Paul writes, "But when God, who had set me apart before I was born and called me through his grace, was pleased to reveal his Son to me, so that I might proclaim him among the Gentiles, I did not confer with any human being." From a persecutor of the early church, Paul has been transformed into a man with a mission to carry the name of Jesus to the Gentile world. At the heart of this transformation is an experience with the risen Christ on the road to Damascus and the belief that in Jesus, God is bringing about the salvation of both Jews and Gentiles. In Galatians, Paul describes his conviction that he has been set apart by God even before he was born and that God's Son has been revealed to him. In language reminiscent of God's word to Jeremiah (1:5)—

> Before I formed you in the womb I knew you,
>   and before you were born I consecrated you;
> I appointed you a prophet to the nations

—Paul expresses his conviction that from the very beginning he has been set apart for a mission. In retrospect and from the vantage point of a Christ-centered faith, Paul assesses the meaning of his own life in terms of God's intention. He is to proclaim Christ among the Gentiles. The one whom Paul did not know, indeed persecuted, has now been revealed to him.

Paul's belief in Christ is both an experience and a conviction, which, in his eyes, allows him to comprehend the "true" meaning of the religion of his people and their sacred texts.[21] Christ and scripture are closely connected for Paul. It is virtually impossible to speak about Paul's reading of scripture apart from his Christology. Christ is the presupposition that Paul brings to his encounter with scripture. It is the revelation of Christ, which he believes he has received, that shapes his understanding of God's people and God's purposes.[22] For Paul, as for many other interpreters of scripture, the Bible is understood to yield its "true" meaning to those who are guided and transformed by the Spirit. To those who stand outside the sphere of the Spirit's activity, the meaning of the scriptures remains hidden.

A New Age

Second Corinthians 3:1–4:6 is one of the most hotly debated and discussed Pauline passages. Whereas many interpreters find in these verses the key to Paul's hermeneutic (letter versus spirit), others reject the hermeneutical interpretation and argue that in fact Paul is engaged primarily in a defense of his ministry. To be sure, Paul is not distinguishing in this text between a literal and a nonliteral reading of scripture (two different principles of interpretation), and his reference to letters of recommendation (3:1–3) is certainly part of an apology for his ministry. But Paul does establish important considerations in this text that affect his understanding of scripture.[23]

Paul writes:

> But their minds were hardened. Indeed, to this very day, when they hear the reading of the old covenant, that same veil is still there, since only in Christ is it set aside. Indeed, to this very day whenever Moses is read, a veil lies over their minds; but when one turns to the Lord, the veil is removed.   (2 Cor. 3:14–15)[24]

My interest in this text focuses on the statement that the minds of the Israelites have been hardened and that the veil, at the reading of the "old covenant," remains to the present time unlifted. This is the only place where Paul seemingly refers to scriptural material as the "old covenant," but if this statement is to be understood, it must also be viewed in light of the discussion in 3:1–11. In these verses, Paul discusses letters of recommendation and distinguishes the "ministry of

death" from the "ministry of the Spirit," which he does by distinguishing between the "written word" (*gramma*) that kills and the Spirit that
makes alive. In this discussion, the "written word" probably signifies
"that which is inscribed" in the text of scripture.[25] Richard Hays writes:
"Just as Christ's epistle is not 'inscribed' (*eggegrammenē*) with ink or on
stone, but written by the Spirit on hearts, so Paul's ministry of the new
covenant is not of the 'script' (*gramma*) but of the Spirit."[26] For Paul,
the "written word" kills, and, in doing so, it belongs to the ministry of
death. The "new covenant," in contrast, is not written on stone but on
human hearts (compare Jer. 31:31–34). Apart from the Spirit and the
transformation of human community (Paul's letter of recommendation is the community and not a mere written text), the words of
scripture are, for Paul, simply script or written text. Scripture rightly
understood, however, is for him *graphē*, and it cannot be rightly
understood apart from the Spirit. As E. Earle Ellis writes: "*Graphē* is
the spirit-carried letter, the Spirit-interpreted letter."[27] Hence, when
Paul in the course of this discussion connects scriptural material with
the "old covenant," he is not implying that scripture in itself is obsolete.
He is claiming that to understand scripture merely as a written text is
to misunderstand it, to have a veil over one's mind. Again Hays writes:
"Thus, though Paul has not set out to discuss hermeneutics, and
although the *gramma/pneuma* distinction is not to be construed as a
juxtaposition of hermeneutical methods, the substance of this passage
indicates that the *diakonia tou pneumatos* [ministry of the Spirit] carries
with it a radically new orientation toward Israel's Scripture."[28]

Paul, in 2 Corinthians 3:4–18, gives the veil two different functions.
In 3:7–11, the implied function of the veil is to conceal the splendor
and glory (impermanent and ineffectual in the light of Christ)[29] of
Moses' face. But in 3:12–18, the veil serves as an image to show that
Moses attempted to conceal from the Israelites the glory of his face and
also to illustrate that the "unbelieving" Jews are hardened (3:14).
When the "old covenant" is read, the veil covers their hearts and
minds. Paul in 3:16 makes clear that in turning to the Lord the veil is
removed. As Moses in Exodus 34:33–34 removed the veil when he
went before the Lord, so now when one turns to the Lord the veil is

lifted. Although Paul does not explicitly say this in 3:12–16, he clearly implies that only through belief in Christ and life in the Spirit can the written text be encountered as scripture (*graphē*).

In 2 Corinthians 4:3–4, Paul relates this to his own ministry and to the gospel: "And even if our gospel is veiled, it is veiled to those who are perishing. In their case the god of this world has blinded the minds of the unbelievers, to keep them from seeing the light of the gospel of the glory of Christ, who is the image of God." For Paul, those who do not believe in Christ are "blinded" and the gospel remains veiled (compare Rom. 11:7–10, 1 Cor. 2:7–10). The implications that this has for the way Paul hears the word of scripture are, of course, manifold.

For Paul, knowledge of the divine purpose is centered in the mystery of God's revelation in Jesus Christ. In Christ, the Spirit is actively revealing the mystery that has been hidden from eternity (Rom. 16:25–26). Thus, Christ becomes the determinant factor in Paul's reassessment of Judaism and his reinterpretation of scripture. Paul does not abandon Judaism or the Jewish scriptures but finds their "true" expression in Christ who for him is the revelation of God. Not only is the future determined christologically for the apostle, but the past can also be correctly discerned only from the perspective of this Christ-mystery. Christology is thus an underlying assumption that enables the apostle to "uncover" the meaning of scripture and relate it to the present as well as to the future. Hence, Paul's conversation with biblical material, as apostle to the Gentiles, takes place at the point where Christology, community, and scripture intersect.

As is typical of sectarian hermeneutics, Paul's conception of scriptural interpretation implies some special knowledge or revelation of divine truth. Moreover, this approach to scripture functions internally to define and establish the theological rationale of an emerging religious community. It is not intended to seek consensus or find common ground with others who share the same scriptural texts. From a sociological point of view, a "Spirit-driven" hermeneutic serves to critique opposing power structures and to revise traditional patterns of religious activity. Paul's revisionist use of the Jewish scriptures was certainly to have this effect. Paul set himself apart from traditional structures of authority, power, and religious identity. Throughout this discussion, however, it is clear that Paul does not view scripture simply as a written text or an object of investigation.

Scripture and the Gospel

In several instances, Paul indicates that either the person of Christ or the gospel can be discerned in scripture. In none of these examples is the biblical text quoted, but direct reference is made to the scriptures, which presupposes that Paul's audience understands that there is some connection between the sacred writings and Christ. Moreover, Paul's reference to the scriptures serves to illustrate, indeed substantiate, the claim that the scriptures point forward to the Messiah. They anticipate his coming. In Jesus, they can be seen to have reached their culmination. The messianic character of the gospel is testified to by the holy scriptures. The sacred tradition itself, according to Paul, points forward to Christ and the gospel.

In the opening of the epistle to the Romans, Paul writes: "Paul, a servant of Jesus Christ, called to be an apostle, set apart for the gospel of God, which he promised beforehand through his prophets in the holy scriptures. . . ." In this introductory statement, Paul brings together the "gospel of God" promised beforehand, prophets, and the holy scriptures. These three elements provide a point of reference for understanding the connection in Pauline thought between scripture and the gospel. God is identified as the originator of the gospel, and the prophets are designated as prophets of God. The gospel originates with God, and it is through God's prophets that it has been promised. The verb "promised beforehand" illustrates the temporal sequence in the apostle's statement (compare 2 Cor. 9:5). For some commentators, this suggests that Paul viewed all of scripture as a prophetic witness to Christ.[30] While this claim may be too strong, it is evident from Romans 1:1–2 that Paul believed that the gospel had been promised through Israel's prophets and that this promise can be found in scripture. Thus, from Paul's point of view and from the point of view of the coming of Jesus, the gospel has been promised beforehand. There is clearly a prospective element in Paul's understanding of scripture as it relates to the gospel. Yet this prospective view is shaped retrospectively

from the vantage point of faith in Christ and the revelation of God's
purposes to Paul.[31]

In Romans 3:21, the scriptures are referred to as "the law and the
prophets."[32] In this text, it is claimed that the "righteousness of God,"
which is testified to by the law and the prophets, has been manifested
apart from the law. Without discussing what is meant by the terms
"righteousness of God" and "gospel of God," it is important to note that
both are connected with Christ. In Romans 1:1–2, however, Christ is the
descendant of David who has been designated Son of God, whereas in
3:21–22 he is the object of faith and the means by which God reveals
divine righteousness. In Romans 1:3, Christ assumes the title of the
Jewish Messiah, Son of David, and is designated by the tradition as Son
of God. This Messiah is identified as the manifestation of God's
righteousness for those who believe in him. He is the culmination, for
the early church, of the expectation that God will bring forth a shoot
from the stump of Jesse. According to Romans 1:1–2 and 3:21–22, the
"gospel of God" has been promised beforehand through the prophets in
the holy scriptures and the "righteousness of God" has been witnessed
to, but only now revealed, by the law and the prophets.

In 1 Corinthians 15:3–4, Paul records the familiar claim that Christ
died for our sins according to the scriptures and that he was buried and
was raised on the third day. This early tradition,[33] which Paul says he
has received, makes the claim that Jesus' death and resurrection were
in accordance with scripture. Paul himself undoubtedly shared this
view, developed in the early tradition of the church, but makes no
attempt to summon passages to illustrate it. This is not to imply that
Paul could not have done so but is a recognition that he was not
compelled by the circumstances of his argument to develop a list of
messianic proof texts. This is, however, another example, indeed the
best example, of a Pauline text that contains a direct reference to
Christ that the apostle has not supported by citing biblical passages,
despite a reference to the scriptures being made. Moreover, the
tradition that Paul says he has received is of such significance that it
can be cited as a reminder of the gospel that the apostle has preached.
That which Paul has received has also been delivered to the Corinthians in the course of the apostle's missionary preaching.

Paul in Galatians 3:8 also makes reference to the gospel having been anticipated in the scriptures when he writes: "And the scripture, foreseeing that God would justify the Gentiles by faith, declared the gospel beforehand to Abraham." Immediately following this statement Paul cites Genesis 12:3 (18:18). In Galatians 3:6–9, the argument focuses primarily on justification and sonship. Thus, the "good news" in this text does not refer directly to Christ but to righteousness and faith. As in Romans 1:2, the prospective character of Paul's understanding of scripture is illustrated; scripture is portrayed as foreseeing. Presumably, Paul means that it can be seen already in scripture that God would justify the Gentiles by faith. The "good news" was announced in advance to Abraham. The manner in which Paul refers to scripture implies that it is an active force as well as an agent of God's power (compare Gal. 3:22). This suggests that the prospective element in the apostle's view of the biblical material rests on a dynamic understanding of scripture and its function. The scriptural material is an agent of God's activity. It has a power and a dynamic quality that reflects the activity of God at work in bringing about the salvation of both Jews and Gentiles.

In each of the Pauline texts discussed in this section, the claim that scripture points forward to Christ is explicit. This, however, is a retrospective view. It is only understood from the vantage point of faith in Christ. The text of scripture itself does not demand that the early church and Paul in particular reach the conclusion that Jesus is testified to by the law and the prophets. This claim only becomes possible once the early church is convinced that Jesus is the Messiah. Apart from this faith conviction, scripture remains mute regarding Jesus. Thus, Paul engages the text of scripture christologically and in the process discovers biblical material that he believes addresses his situation as apostle to the Gentiles.

The conversation model of interpretation is clearly reflected in Paul's approach to and encounter with scripture. The interpretive voice of the apostle and the text of the Bible encounter each other and, as we shall see, result in interpretive conclusions that may well have seemed astonishing to Paul's Jewish contemporaries. It is clear that Paul's "Spirit-driven" sense of biblical interpretation has a sectarian

religious quality about it. Yet it is also the case that the messianic
character of Paul's gospel is related to the sacred tradition of scripture
and is proclaimed as a universal message according to the principle of
faith. Paul, the sectarian Jew, proclaims a gospel message that also
reaches beyond traditional religious boundaries. But before we proceed further, an important characteristic of Paul's exegesis in the
epistles must be illustrated.

Exegesis and Christology

In the book of Acts, Luke makes two explicit statements regarding
Paul's use of scripture. In 17:2–3, he writes: "And on three sabbath
days [he] argued with them from the scriptures, explaining and
proving that it was necessary for the Messiah to suffer and to rise from
the dead, and saying, 'This is the Messiah, Jesus whom I am
proclaiming to you.' " Likewise, in 28:23 Luke writes: "From morning
until evening He explained the matter to them, testifying to the
kingdom of God and trying to convince them about Jesus both from
the law of Moses and from the prophets." There is no compelling
reason to think that Paul did not do this during the course of his
missionary work, but in the epistles he does not use scriptural
quotations in this way. The addressees of his letters are already
followers of Christ. They do not need to be convinced that Jesus is the
Messiah. This is a conviction that Paul and the people to whom he is
writing hold in common. The apostle, however, is compelled to work
out the implications of what it means for both Jews and Gentiles that
salvation is by "faith" and not "works."

When compared to the total number of Paul's biblical citations,
those direct quotations that are explicitly christological in terms of
content are limited.[34] Almost four out of ten of Paul's direct quotations
are related to justification by faith, sonship, freedom from the law,
and, in general, the relationship between Jews and Gentiles. These
Pauline discussions, of course, rest on a messianic presupposition, but
they are concerned primarily with faith as the basis of righteousness.
Almost one-fourth of Paul's quotations deal with ethical or wisdom-
related topics, while the remainder of the citations are scattered

among a variety of subjects. What this illustrates is that Paul's view of the relationship between scripture and Christ—a view presumably held by most in the early church—is not worked out exegetically or elaborated in his epistles. In fact, only a few biblical citations are directly applied to the figure of Christ.[35]

Historical and Theological Paradigms

The topic of Paul's context also raises a larger interpretive issue for us concerning historical and theological paradigms. The conclusion that an interpreter of Paul draws regarding the apostle's relation to Judaism affects the way Pauline texts are understood. But the question of paradigms extends well beyond the way Paul is perceived in relation to Judaism. In fact, the way an interpreter understands Christian origins in general affects the way New Testament texts are read. Hence, judgments about Paul's context are affected by the perception of Christian origins that is brought to bear on the reading of Pauline texts. Needless to say, the effect of these perceptions on the interpretation of Paul are examined too infrequently.

Three paradigms are of concern to us. The first of these is really a Christian theological view but one that has historical and exegetical implications. I shall refer to it as the "replacement model" of Christian origins. In the history of salvation, the "old Israel" has been replaced by the "new Israel." The old covenant has been superseded by the new covenant. This model of Christian origins has a long and insidious history in the development of Christianity. It has been the seedbed from which Christian anti-Judaism has sprung, and it has reinforced a line of Pauline interpretation that at the very least has depreciated Judaism, the law, and the place of the Jewish scriptures in the development of the apostle's theology. This model manifests itself in different ways, but it can certainly be detected in the suggestion that Paul was tortured by the burdens of the Mosaic law, sought to escape from the legalistic religion of his ancestors, and ultimately found liberation in Christ. To use E. P. Sanders's terminology again, those who suggest that Paul, religiously speaking, moved from "plight" to "solution" exhibit a form of this thinking.[36] The most common interpretive result of this model is to see Paul as someone who is antithetical to Judaism.

However, the "replacement model" finds little support in the epistles themselves. Paul never refers to a "new Israel." As we have seen, he does not reject the goodness of the law, and he does not understand the promises of God to have been abrogated. In other words, Paul does not view Christ as God's rejection of Israel and its covenant.[37] Moreover, if Paul had understood the way of "faith" to be a rejection of God's covenant with Israel, he would have had no basis upon which to argue that Abraham is the progenitor of the people of "faith." This is not to argue that Paul sees no tension between Israel and Christ. It is to claim, however, that any dissonance that Paul finds between the two is inherent in his messianism and his apocalypticism, both of which are anchored in Judaism. This means that the apostle's religion is closest in form and type to sectarian Judaism.

The second paradigm I shall call the "offshoot model" of Christian origins. In other words, the Christian community has branched off from Judaism, which is an ancient but ongoing religious phenomenon. This is a model or paradigm that has both theological and exegetical implications. It suggests that the Pauline religious community has been given birth and nurtured by Judaism but that it developed in such a way that it would eventually separate itself from historic Judaism. Paul himself gives some indication that he views the Gentile mission in these terms when he refers to the analogy of the olive branch. However, even in this analogy, the apostle appears to say that the Gentile mission is not a splinter phenomenon but something incorporated into Israel. That which is "wild" has been made to share the richness of that which is "tame." As we have noted, this preserves the theological primacy of Israel. But it does not by itself provide historical support for the "offshoot model" of Christian origins.

Perhaps the most significant support for this view is supplied when the concept of justification by faith is seen in the context of the Gentile mission. Thus, the problem of how one qualifies to be part of the community of Christ is really part of the larger issue of the identity of the people of God. As we shall see below, the question of identity plays an important role in Paul's discussion of Abraham's faith and righteousness.[38] The redefinition of the people of God by Paul and other followers of Christ is related to sectarian Jewish attempts to redefine the parameters of the community. The fact that Paul sought admission to this community for Gentiles ultimately meant that this fellowship would separate from Judaism. The sociology of this increasingly Gentile community would ensure that an independent religion was finally established. In other words, Pauline religion dealt with a typical Jewish concern: "What does it mean to be the people of God?" But it did so in a way that could not in the end be maintained within historic Judaism.

The primary historical problem, it is argued, with the "offshoot model" is that it suggests a greater degree of continuity between early Judaism and rabbinic Judaism than can be maintained by the literary sources. Therefore, a third paradigm has been proposed. I shall refer to it as the "sibling model." The claim is that first-century Judaism has given rise to two great religious phenomena, rabbinic Judaism and Christianity. Both are transformations of different strands of early Jewish religion.[39] Early Christianity is not so much a breakaway phenomenon as it is a transformation of a portion of first-century Judaism. Early on, it began to appropriate to itself alien characteristics. Over time, Christianity and rabbinic Judaism went in very different directions.

The advantage of this paradigm for understanding Paul is that both his letters and his emerging theology can be viewed in the context of religious transformation and evolution, as the apostle sought to recenter his religious worldview in light of Christ. Moreover, this model takes seriously the religious transformation that ultimately gave rise to rabbinic Judaism. As the title of Alan Segal's book *Rebecca's Children* suggests, the formation of Christianity and Judaism is analogous to the birth of the twin children Jacob and Esau. They fought even in the womb but both claim common parentage.

If the "replacement model" is the least appropriate way of viewing Paul's relation to Judaism, the "sibling model" is the most accurate historically and fruitful interpretively. It allows Paul's religion to be understood in terms of sectarian Judaism. At the same time, it can account for the fact that Christianity very early moved beyond the

confines of Israel. In addition, it avoids the error of thinking that
nothing of significance occurred in Judaism after the first century. It
also gives us an opportunity to see Paul's conversation with scripture in
the context of an evolutionary religious transformation, which takes
seriously his abiding theological relationship with Judaism. This
abiding theological relationship is fundamental to Paul's historical
context and his encounter with the biblical text.

Conclusion

The divine mystery that has been revealed to Paul in Christ opens
new ways for reading and listening to the ancient texts of the Jewish
people. Paul's concern is not simply to establish the historical details of
a scriptural passage, or to ponder the "written word," or to determine
the intent of the biblical writer, but to show, as a man of faith, how the
sacred text testifies to his, as well as to his audiences' conviction that in
Christ the new age has come to pass (2 Cor. 5:16–17). This is clearly
the perspective of a religious man who believes that he has been given
a vision of God's plan for the salvation of the world. Paul's understanding of the christological mystery grounded in the community of faith
(the church) thus becomes determinative for his reading of the sacred
scriptures. In turn, the scriptures speak to him about what it means to
be a child of Abraham and a member of the body of Christ.

The traditions of the early church, that is, the traditions regarding
the messiahship of Jesus, grew out of and alongside the religious
traditions of the Jews much as traditions had done in Judaism for
centuries. With time, the entrance point for biblical interpretation
became not merely the text of scripture or Jewish interpretations of
scripture but the way the text had come to be understood within the
Christian community. Alongside the sacred text of scripture, there
developed a normative body of tradition that exerted its own influence
over the way the biblical material was to be understood. The dynamic
of this process had been in place in Judaism for generations. What
made this process distinctive within the Christian community, however, was the fact that the anticipated Messiah was believed now to
have come, been crucified, raised from the dead, and seated on the

throne of God from which he would make salvation available to both Jews and Gentiles. The early Christian approach to interpretation was in many ways Jewish, but the results that were produced led first to a reevaluation of what Judaism was and eventually to a split between the church and the synagogue. This reevaluation and eventual split stem ultimately from the church's christological presuppositions and Gentile mission.

Paul accepted the early church's conclusion that Christ was the son of David, and he was certainly not hesitant about using the christological formulations that had developed in those first decades following Jesus' death. There is evidence that these formulations had themselves become part of the tradition to which Paul attributed authority and which shaped his view of Jesus' messiahship. In their inception, they were part of the oral tradition of the church; later, they established themselves as part of the authoritative proclamation of the community and entered into its written tradition. That Jesus' messiahship was in accordance with the scriptures became not only the claim of the early church but also one of its fundamental presuppositions. From that point in the development of the tradition, it was sufficient simply to remind the readers of an epistle, as Paul did, that Jesus is the Messiah who was attested to by the scriptures. As we can see from the letter to the Hebrews, this way of relating scripture and Christology was not the only option available to a writer of early Christian epistles. However, unless the circumstances of a particular letter demanded a messianic exegetical discussion, it probably would have been considered superfluous.

But the gospel of "righteousness by faith" is for Paul a topic of great urgency. This issue and the problems that have resulted from Paul's stand on the matter require direct attention. The apostle must defend himself and his position. He must attempt to show that his position is grounded in sacred scripture and authoritative tradition. All the tools at Paul's disposal must be summoned to develop and present the case that he is compelled by circumstances to make. Since he is breaking new ground, he cannot rely on traditions previously developed. He must use his own ingenuity to forge a new way of looking at the manner in which God has made Israel a light to the Gentiles. In doing this, Paul is at his most creative. He is not simply a conduit for the tradition but one who makes tradition. Paul's effect on the history of Christian theological formation speaks eloquently for his ingenuity, if not also for his persuasiveness. This is not to say that even at his most creative Paul is not working with a vast array of prior tradition, but it is to argue that at significant points he moves into the realm of the unexplored. He seeks to make theological connections that had not yet been formulated. He strives to address the problems that confront the fledgling churches in the Gentile lands, and he works to maintain the unity of the body of Christ.

Paul is a missionary and to the support of that effort he devotes his intellectual energy. The apostle does not do systematic theology nor does he do his theological work in a vacuum. He is engaged in the task of bringing the gospel to the Gentile world. That is his commission, and that is the driving force behind his application of Jewish categories of thought to the service of a message that is rapidly moving out from under the protective wing of its parent religious community. The further the church moves beyond the confines of Judaism, the more it is required to develop its own categories of religious thought, to shape a new view of the world, and to adopt forms of expressing the gospel that will communicate meaningfully to an increasingly non-Jewish audience. In this process, Paul is a crucial link, for he seeks to bring the message of Jesus, a Jew by birth, to the world of the Roman Empire.

III

Testified to by the Law and the Prophets: The Voice of Scripture

The Words of Sacred Scripture

To argue that scripture is a partner in the interpretive conversation requires that we acknowledge at least two important facts: the record of that conversation has been preserved only by Paul, and it has been preserved only in literary form. Thus, the voice of scripture in the interpretive conversation can only be discerned by examining Paul's epistles. In this section, we shall seek to discover the voice of scripture in the writings of Paul. The objective is not merely to identify technical details for their own sake but to see the way these literary features of Paul's citations enhance our understanding of the apostle's encounter with the sacred text—especially the contribution of the sacred text to the interpretive conversation. The implications of this contribution will become fully apparent only in chapters IV through VII. In these four chapters, we will extend the insights of chapters II and III to specific Pauline conversations with biblical material.

Structure

If we look closely at Paul's biblical quotations and their literary contexts in the epistles, we find a basic pattern. It consists of three parts: (1) opening statement, (2) introductory formula, and (3) scriptural citation. In its simplest form, this type of reference includes neither an explanation of the biblical text nor an elaboration of themes related directly to it. The citation serves as a source of religious authority, and it substantiates the statement that has been made. The interpretive value is found in the connection drawn between the scriptural passage and the opening statement. A simple example will be sufficient to illustrate this point. In Romans 1:16–17, the apostle writes: "For I am not ashamed of the gospel; it is the power of God for salvation to everyone who has faith, to the Jew first and also to the Greek. For in it the righteousness of God is revealed through faith for faith." Following the expression of thanksgiving in verses 8–15, Paul writes these words. In the literary context of Romans 1:16–17, they function as the opening statement. Habakkuk 2:4 is then introduced ("as it is written") and quoted ("The one who is righteous will live by faith"). The purpose of the biblical citation is to confirm the opening statement, and the force of the quotation is directed toward that purpose. There is no direct explication of the Habakkuk text in Romans 1:18–23. On the contrary, the course of the discussion shifts following the quotation.

This type of citation is often referred to as a "proof text." The text is used to confirm an assertion that the writer has made. In one sense, this is exactly what happens. The opening statement is substantiated by the biblical quotation. However, a word of caution is necessary. Undue emphasis on the proof-text form tends to limit our ability to perceive the voice of scripture and its contribution to the interpretive dialogue. The term "proof text" might imply that scripture was simply an authoritative record to which Paul turned to prove his arguments and not also a source of edification, verbal stimulation, and inspiration. For Jews, scripture was sacred and holy (Rom. 1:2). It was a source of inspiration for life, an expression of the will of God, and a basis for interpretation and religious argumentation. Thus, I note that in Romans 1:16–17 Paul has used the words "righteousness" and "faith." These key words appear in the opening statement, and they (or different forms of these words) also appear in the Habakkuk citation. This suggests that Paul has conceived the opening assertion in light of the scriptural quotation that he intended to cite. It is also probable that the discussion in Romans 1:16–17 is developed against the background of Genesis 15:6 (Abraham "believed the LORD; and the

LORD reckoned it to him as righteousness") and Paul's previous discussions of justification by faith.

Variations of this basic threefold pattern are also found. For example, instead of citing just one biblical passage, the apostle can string a series of passages together (see Rom. 3:9–18; 9:24–29; 10:18–21; 11:7–10; and 15:8–12). The pattern is essentially the same as in the simple form, but in this case the argument has been enhanced and developed by the addition of scriptural passages. Other modifications of the basic threefold pattern include an elaboration, interpretation, or application of the biblical reference following the quotation. At the end of the quotation, the apostle appends a statement that relates directly to the biblical text. In this way, the biblical text feeds thematically and verbally into the formulation of the ensuing discussion. In other words, the force of the quotation is not directed only toward the opening statement.[1]

The elaboration that follows a quotation frequently involves the weaving together of words and ideas from the passage. In other instances, Paul introduces his interpretation or application of the biblical text with a transition word or phrase ("so too," "for whatever," "thus," "it was written for our sake," "now therefore," etc.).[2] This indicates that Paul intends to make his interpretation or application of the text explicit. In still other cases, the apostle attaches an exhortation to the quotation (see especially Rom. 12:19–20; 1 Cor. 3:19–21; 2 Cor. 6:16–7:1).

Before we look more closely at some specific examples, it is important to consider a number of the implications that are central to the discussion so far. It is evident that scriptural quotations are often imposed on the discussion in order to illustrate or enhance the argument. To be sure, this is not always the case, but to the extent that a biblical citation is used as a "proof text," it is lifted from its original literary context and interjected into a new literary context for the purpose of enhancing the argument. In the transfer from one literary context to another, Paul certainly manipulates the meaning of the biblical citation. He apparently does so on the assumption that what is "true" in the biblical context is also "true" in the context of his specific presentation. Hence, Paul's readers are to associate the "truth" of the biblical text with the "truth" of a particular set of ideas that are being communicated to them. In this regard, the context of the apostle and his literary presentation are ultimately determinative for the way the biblical citation is understood. The value of the biblical text is found in that which it can contribute to the apostle's ability to communicate a set of ideas to his readers.

"Proof text," in the modern use of scripture, is widely deplored and considered inappropriate. It distorts the interpretive conversation by failing to take seriously the context and integrity of the biblical text. What should be a dialogue becomes in effect a monologue. To the extent that Paul engages in simple "proof text," his technique of using scripture is inadequate for modern interpreters. Our sense of literary and historical "truth" is such that interpretive meaning is discovered in context. For the modern interpreter to disregard context is to engage in an unsophisticated form of conversation. Yet I do know people who use scripture in precisely this way and for whom "proof text" is considered entirely appropriate. The "proof text" use of scriptural citations does not necessarily mean that a conversation with scripture is not going on. It does mean, according to most modern standards of interpretation in context, that only one partner in the conversation is speaking. Before long this form of conversation can become very dull.

Still, from a literary point of view, I have suggested that Paul's use of scripture cannot be described adequately by the term "proof text." The biblical passage makes its own contribution to the apostle's presentation. Both verbally and thematically the citation informs the way the discussion proceeds. In this way, the biblical text imposes itself on the writer. This does not mean that the original context of the biblical passage is of ultimate concern to Paul, but it does mean that the literary integrity of the passage is maintained and utilized in the formulation of the discussion. Therefore, the scriptural text is not simply a literary vehicle in the act of communication but is instrumental in the development of that which is communicated. The scriptural text functions both as a literary and a theological agent. In other words, it assists Paul in the literary construction of his epistles as well as in the process of theological conceptualization. This will become clearer as we proceed.

Interpretation and Application

As we have observed, Paul in a number of examples makes explicit his application of scriptural material. At the conclusion of the discussion in Romans 4, the apostle in 4:23–24 writes: "Now the words, 'it was reckoned to him,' were written not for his sake alone, but for ours also." The words "it was reckoned to him" are depicted in Genesis as being spoken about Abraham. But in Romans they are applied to those who believe in the one who raised Jesus from the dead. Similarly, Paul applies the Sarah/Hagar material in Galatians 4:21–31 to his own historical and literary context. He writes in Galatians 4:29: "But just as at that time the child who was born according to the flesh persecuted the child who was born according to the Spirit, so it is now also." To this statement, Paul appends a citation from Genesis 21:10: "Drive out the slave and her child; for the child of the slave will not share the inheritance with the child of the free woman." To make explicit his application of the scriptural material, Paul continues: "So then, friends, we are children, not of the slave but of the free woman." Finally, in 1 Corinthians 9:9–10 Paul writes: "For it is written in the law of Moses, 'You shall not muzzle an ox while it is treading out the grain.' Is it for oxen that God is concerned? Or does he not speak entirely for our sake? It was indeed written for our sake." The context of this statement has to do with Paul's apostolic right to receive material support. It is to this situation that Paul has applied the citation. This is another example of the way a scriptural reference has come to address a contemporary controversy.[3]

In all three of these examples, the application of the biblical text is made explicit. The force of the scriptural passage aids in the process of visualizing and defining the nature of the problem that confronts Paul, as well as in the act of communicating this vision to his audience. The biblical text conjures up images for Paul, and these images are instrumental in communicating with his readers. If righteousness was reckoned to Abraham by faith, that same paradigm can also be applied to those who live by "faith" in the present. Likewise, if there is conflict between those who live by "faith" and those who demand obedience to the law of Moses, that conflict can be defined in terms of the biblical paradigm in which there is seen to be conflict between Sarah and Hagar, Isaac and Ishmael. Moreover, the child of the slave (the one who demands obedience to the law) will not inherit with the child of the free woman (the one who lives by "faith"). That which is "true" in scripture is "true" in the present. At the point where the text of sacred scripture defines Paul's sense of his own situation and the problems that confront him, the biblical text and the apostolic context have merged. This clearly seems to be the case in the examples that we have cited. To say that Paul has interpreted the biblical texts for his own purposes is certainly true, but this is an incomplete description of the way he engages the scriptural material.

In other contexts, Paul turns to scripture for its instructive and edifying value. Following the citation of Psalm 69:9 in Romans 15:3, Paul writes: "For whatever was written in former days was written for our instruction, so that by steadfastness and by the encouragement of the scriptures we might have hope" (v. 4). The advice that Paul gives to the Romans is that the strong should bear the failings of the weak. He exhorts his readers to build up their neighbors. As an example, Christ did not please himself. On the contrary, he suffered reproach, as it is written in scripture. In this context, scripture is portrayed as having both an instructive and an edifying function. The things that were written in former times serve to encourage the community and to engender hope in the present. Paul understands scripture as having the ability to sustain him and his readers. The value and authority of the things that were written in the past continue to prevail in the present. In other words, time has not rendered scripture obsolete. It still functions as a voice for the instruction and edification of the community. Even among those followers of Christ in Rome, the words of the psalmist serve to sustain in the face of difficulty. They are words that speak of Christ, according to Paul, and they remind his readers of the reproach that Christ suffered. Through Paul, the words of the psalmist are intended to communicate a message of consolation and steadfastness. The literary link between the word of scripture and the community in Rome is, of course, the epistle. It is the vehicle through which the community encounters a message of encouragement.

In 1 Corinthians 10:1–13, the apostle reminds his readers of Israel's experience in the wilderness. He announces that the things that happened in Sinai are examples or warnings for them in the present. The discussion in 10:6–13 is primarily ethical, as Paul warns the Corinthians against idolatry, immorality, putting the Lord to the test, and grumbling. He relates the wilderness stories to his ethical concern by stating: "These things happened to them to serve as an example, and they were written down to instruct us, on whom the ends of the ages have come" (10:11). The scriptural material functions as a source of instruction and guidance for those who live in the "end time." The way Paul words his statement indicates that his perspective of the "end time" is an important factor in discerning the ethical significance and value of scripture for his religious community. As we saw in chapter II, the apostle sees scripture in light of the revelation of Christ. From the vantage point of Christ and the "uncovering" of God's purposes in him, the scriptures are read and listened to differently. Likewise, this retrospective view has ethical significance for the community of Christ. The scriptures are instructive for the way the people of Christ are to act.[4]

Both pastorally and ethically, the scriptures have instructive value. In his absence, Paul has used them to guide and support those to whom he is writing. We do not know the effect these exhortations and words of encouragement had on his readers. But we do know that Paul sought from afar to sustain his readers in hope. Through reference to the sacred writings of his people, the apostle tried to build up the community of Christ. Not only was biblical material used to formulate and communicate theological arguments, it was used as an instrument for the religious edification and guidance of those who shared his faith in Christ.

In addition to theological arguments and ethical guidance, Paul also uses biblical material for allegorical purposes. Though many Pauline texts have been described as being allegorical,[5] only in Galatians 4:24 does Paul actually use a form of the word "allegory." From the literary context of the argument in Galatians 4:21–31, it is clear that Paul uses a form of this word to indicate that he intends to draw out the meaning and significance of the biblical material that is referred to in 4:22–23. Regarding the translation of the word *allēgoroumena*, Ernest D. Burton argued that it should be rendered "which things are allegorical utterances."[6] He goes on to argue that the implication of this grammatical construction is that Paul is speaking of the passage's meaning in the present context and not what it meant originally.[7] According to Burton, *allēgoreō* in Galatians 4:24 can mean "to utter something which has another meaning than that of the words taken literally."[8] The only other possibility in this context, according to Burton, is "to draw out the spiritual meaning supposed to underlie the words in their literal sense."[9] H. D. Betz has suggested that the term *allēgoroumena* ought to be translated: "These things have an allegorical meaning."[10] He also argues that the linguistic evidence and the nature of the argument in Galatians 4:21–31 both indicate that Paul has approached the use of the scriptural material in this text allegorically. Paul has intended to draw out the correct interpretation, which he believes underlies a superficial reading of the biblical narrative.[11]

Whether or not the term "allegory" is adequate to describe Paul's use of scripture in texts other than Galatians 4:21–31 is not of concern to us. It must be noted, however, that in Galatians Paul has not extracted, as did the great Jewish allegorist Philo, elaborate cosmological and religious lessons from the biblical words or events. Paul has uncovered what he considers to be the "true" meaning of the Abrahamic material and has applied this specifically to the context of the argument in Galatians. Thus, there is a convergence in the use of scriptural material in Galatians 4:21–31 between the literary world of Paul's text and the meaning ascribed to the story of Sarah and Hagar in Genesis. To state this more broadly, the material from Genesis that has been selected by Paul has been made to speak to the historical, theological, and literary concerns of the apostle. In establishing this conformity between the text of scripture and its context in the epistle, Paul has used allegory to forge a connection between the narrative of Genesis and the church's historical situation in Galatia, the apostle's own theological framework, and the literary coherence of the letter. To the extent that Paul has been successful in establishing a congruity between text and context on these three levels, he has also illustrated for us the basic spheres within which sacred texts function in the lives of religious communities: (1) historical, (2) theological/religious, and (3) literary. Allegory as a form of conversation with the biblical text has a long tradition in the history of biblical interpretation but, once again, in most contexts in which scripture is used today allegory is thought to be an inadequate form of conversation. It clearly is a method of engaging the text, but a method that in most cases does not fit within modern "circles of plausibility."

Verbal Generation

I have already noted that Paul uses key words to relate biblical passages and elaborate theological themes. In this section, I shall develop this claim and look in greater detail at the way the apostle uses certain words to generate and shape his literary presentations. Out of the entire corpus of Pauline letters, Romans 9–11 illustrates this characteristic most vividly. This section of the epistle to the Romans provides the best example of verbal generation. First of all, these three chapters constitute a sustained discussion on the issue of the Jews and their place in the plan of God. Second, these chapters are filled with scriptural quotations. Third, the issue under discussion is so troublesome for Paul that he must draw on all of his biblical and theological resources to maintain the image of a trustworthy God, while at the same time holding to the notion that God justifies the ungodly through faith in Christ. For these reasons, Romans 9–11 will provide the focus for the discussion.[12]

In Romans 9:7, a word that appears in the Greek text of Genesis 21:12 becomes formative for Paul in this chapter. That word is the Greek verb which means "to call." In the New Revised Standard Version of Romans 9:7, this verb is translated "named." This rendering is not incorrect, but it obscures the verbal connections based on this word. Paul writes: "And not all of Abraham's children are his true descendants; but 'It is through Isaac that descendants shall be named [literally: called] for you.' " On the theological and religious level, this is Paul's way of seeking to distinguish "Israel from Israel" and "true descendants" from "children." On the literary level, this verb will become instrumental in shaping the ensuing discussion in chapter 9. It is important to note that this word has been injected into Paul's presentation by the scriptural text.

In Romans 9:12 the participial form of this same verb appears. Paul writes: "Even before they had been born or had done anything good or bad (so that God's purpose of election might continue, not by works but by his call) . . ." (9:11–12). The verb "to call" in the quotation in verse 7 and the participial form of this same word in verse 12 give us a clue to the reason why Paul has differentiated "works" and the "call" rather than the expected "works" and "faith." According to the apostle's sense of logic, since Abraham's descendants are named (called) through Isaac, it follows that Jacob's election takes place through the call of God and not through merit. What emerges on a theological level is a concept of the call of God as it relates to the people of Israel. But it can be seen that this concept is generated by a play on the verb "to call."

If this were the only instance of this word or this technique in Paul's discussion, one might be inclined to say that this verbal link is simply coincidental. However, that is not the case. Later in the discussion, in verse 24, Paul once again uses the verb "to call": ". . . including us whom he has called, not from the Jews only but also from the Gentiles." Once again, Paul has drawn on the verb "to call" in order to articulate an aspect of his argument. Not only have the Jews been called but so have the Gentiles. Furthermore, if one looks closely at the Greek text of Hosea 2:23, which Paul cites in 9:25, one finds that the prophetic text reads "I shall say" rather than "I shall call" as it has been rendered in Romans. This variation may be due to the fact that Paul has followed the text of an undiscovered Greek manuscript. But the more likely explanation is that Paul has simply altered the text of Hosea to make it reflect a verbal link with the adjacent citation from Hosea 1:10 in which the verb "to call" does appear and to make it conform to the literary pattern that we have identified.

A similar example of verbal generation appears in Romans 10:19 and 11:11. In chapter 11, the apostle rearranges the order of salvation-history. On account of the trespass of Israel, the message of salvation has now gone forth to the Gentiles. The purpose of the Gentile mission is to make Israel jealous. This is certainly an interesting twist to the generally accepted order of salvation. One can see that this rearrangement is an attempt on Paul's part to justify the legitimacy of the Gentile mission and to give meaning to the Jews' "unbelief."[13] The "jealousy" motif is critical in Paul's argument. When we look at the literary context of this discussion, we find that the word "to make jealous" is actually interjected into the presentation in Romans 10:19. Paul cites Deuteronomy 32:21: "I will make you jealous of those who are not a nation; with a foolish nation I will make you angry." Hence, it is the scriptural text itself that brings the verb "to make jealous" into the discussion. It is certainly true that the meaning of Deuteronomy 32:21 lends itself to the interpretation that Paul has placed upon the text, but it also appears to be the case that the verb "to make jealous" has served as an agent in the stimulation of Paul's thinking. Those who are not a nation (Gentiles) will be God's tool in making Israel jealous. Once again, we can see the way in which the text of a scriptural passage has assisted Paul in generating his discussion.

A final example from Paul's discourse in these chapters will suffice to illustrate our point. In Romans 10:12–13, Paul writes: "For there is no distinction between Jew and Greek; the same Lord is Lord of all and is generous to all who call on [upon] him. For, 'Everyone who calls on [upon] the name of the Lord shall be saved.' " We note immediately that a cognate form of the verb "to call" (literally "to call upon") appears in the citation from Joel 2:32. In this context, the emphasis is not on the call of God but on calling upon God. For our purposes, the important feature is the way the apostle has used the verb "to call upon" as the basis for constructing a series of interlocking questions. He writes: "But how are they to call on [upon] one in whom they have not believed? And how are they to believe in one of whom they have never heard? And how are they to hear without someone to proclaim him? And how are they to proclaim him unless they are sent?" Through the repetition of words, Paul has constructed a series of deliberative questions that move from the notion of calling upon God to the sending of preachers. In each case, the second member of the preceding question is repeated.

First Member	*Second Member*
1. Call upon	1. Believe
2. Believe	2. Heard
3. Hear	3. Preacher
4. Preach	4. Sent

From a literary point of view, this is certainly a case of verbal generation. The apostle has used the technique of literary repetition to drive the argument forward.

In Romans 10:14–15, the scriptural text itself has provided the impetus for the discussion. However, Paul can use this same technique without citing a biblical passage. In Romans 8:30, he writes: "And those whom he predestined he also called; and those whom he called he also justified; and those whom he justified he also glorified." Similarly, in Romans 5:3–4 he states: "And not only that, but we also boast in our sufferings, knowing that suffering produces endurance, and endurance produces character, and character produces hope, and hope does not disappoint us." This pattern of verbal repetition clearly plays a role in Paul's literary style of presentation, and as we have seen, this technique can be triggered by a scriptural text.

Summary

In these pages, I have sought to illustrate the instrumentality of scripture from a literary and verbal point of view. It should be clear by now that scripture not only generates concepts and categories but contributes literarily to the formation of religious thought patterns and to the process of written communication. It should be noted, however, that verbal generation and repetition based on texts of scripture may have been born in the first instance of oral, not written, communication. As Paul preached and debated among the people of the Diaspora, these rhetorical patterns and repetitive ways of using words were enhanced and honed. People heard the apostle weave texts together and play with key words.[14]

When he wrote his epistles, these techniques were simply carried over into the written medium. For those who now read the epistles, the euphonic patterns would have been replaced by the visual linking of words. The sense of sound would have been replaced by the sight of words scrawled on some kind of writing material. Just as preachers today understand the change that takes place when a sermon that is intended to be heard is written out and distributed to interested parishioners, so one can understand the change in the dynamic between Paul's preaching and his letters. But Paul's letters were undoubtedly also read aloud in the communities to which they were addressed. In that way, they would have continued to function as oral forms of communication. Euphonic patterns and repetition may well have been designed to capture the hearers' attention and to impress them with significant details. In any case, Paul's interaction with the Bible is carried out against a background of oral communication.

It is also clear that the distinction between oral and written communication is intimately tied up with the formation and production of the Bible, the means and methods of transmitting the sacred traditions, and the manner in which these texts and traditions are used by subsequent individuals and communities. Hence, the interpreter of the Pauline letters must necessarily be concerned with the art of human communication as the sacred texts of the community's tradition move back and forth between oral and written expression. In that sense, the Pauline letters are the literary residue of the apostle's interaction with the churches in Gentile lands. Only subsequently did Christianity elevate these letters themselves to the rank of sacred scripture. That fact determined in large measure the way these writings were to be read, used, and studied by future generations.

Based on the discussion to this point, it is clear that Paul did not—could not—have a concern for modern hermeneutical theory or exegetical technique. Moreover, he does not appear to have been seriously concerned with the authorial intention of the biblical writers, and he gives no clue that he understands the meaning of biblical texts to be a matter of discerning the historical context of the Bible. However, he does display some concern for literary context, as the discussion of Abraham's circumcision in Romans 4 indicates. But, on the whole, these kinds of concerns are modern concerns. They are concerns born of Enlightenment ideas about meaning, knowledge, and truth. They are part of the modern interpretive context, and they govern the way modern critical conversations with scripture are structured. Whereas Paul might consider it appropriate to allegorize scripture or to summon a "proof text," modern critical readers of the Bible consider this an inappropriate way of discerning the meaning of the biblical text. Methodologically it is inappropriate, and it does not lead to conclusions about the text that are considered plausible.

On the other hand, Paul considers the text of scripture to be dynamic. It is not merely something to be apprehended but is to be fused with the central convictions of his religion and theology. He builds on the words and images of the text, and he brings these words and images to bear on the argument at hand. Images merge and coalesce as Paul seeks to bring the meaning of scripture to light in the context of the Gentile mission. Indeed, scripture assists Paul in forming and generating his pattern of theological argumentation. From the perspective of an apocalyptically shaped theology and Christology, Paul encounters scripture. As one called to be an apostle to the Gentiles, he approaches scripture with the conviction that he has received God's revelation. For him, the Spirit opens the meaning of the scriptures and reveals the purposes of God.

It is not fair to say, however, that Paul's conversation with scripture has simply degenerated into a monologue. But it is true that scriptural text and interpretive context do come closely together and begin to merge. The concerns and images of the one affect the concerns and images of the other. That which is "true" in scripture is "true" in the present. And by implication, that which is "true" in the present is "true" in scripture. Because Paul is not concerned with a historical-critical reading of the biblical text, he is not impressed by the historical divide that separates the biblical text from him and his context. He approaches the biblical text both as a text and as a voice, and properly understood it is the revelation of God. Thus, the goal of interpretation as such is not to discern the biblical writer's intention or to discover the meaning of the biblical text in its historical context but to ascertain the message of God. In effect, that comes about by bringing the scriptural text into parallel with Paul's own religious and interpretive context. While modern historical-critical interpreters of biblical texts may find themselves at odds with the Bible because of the historical divide that is perceived to separate them from the world of the Bible, the apostle apparently senses little or no conflict between the text, understood correctly, and his own context. But for Paul the biblical text itself becomes instrumental in making sense out of the present context. As we shall see below, this is displayed most vividly in the way Paul engages scripture in order to deal with the problem of the Gentiles and their inclusion in the community of Christ. It is also displayed, however, in Paul's perception of the Jews and their abiding place in the purposes of God.

There is little wonder that Paul's theology and his interpretation of scripture were considered offensive to most of his Jewish contemporaries. For example, to claim that Abraham is an example of faith that signals that Gentiles can become part of the community apart from the law is certainly not self-evident from the text. In the story of Abraham Paul claims to find something about the structure of redemptive reality. Inclusion in the community of Christ, and thus salvation, is by faith and not works. But for most Jews of his day, this would clearly have been considered outside the "circle of plausibility." The story of Abraham has to do with covenant and the identity of the covenant people. It is not about inclusion of Gentiles, and it is not about faith righteousness as opposed to law righteousness. But Paul's arguments about inclusion of Gentiles and faith righteousness were ultimately to have a profound effect on the development of the early church. The Jesus movement burst forth beyond the boundaries of Judaism, and Christianity became primarily a Gentile phenomenon. Paul's theology and his rereading of the Genesis texts were to have a normative function in the life of the church. They were to become canonical.

Having looked at Paul's biblical citations in terms of their structure, their application in context, and their generative value, we have now made the first steps toward understanding the way Paul hears the words of scripture. In the interpretive conversation, Paul both speaks and listens. He addresses scripture and is addressed by it. As we have observed, the contribution of scripture to this encounter can be seen already in the technical features of Paul's quotations from scripture. These insights must now be broadened and extended.

Scripture and the Voice of Tradition

Paul's conversation with scripture involves more than a simple encounter between the text of scripture and the apostle's own personal religious conviction. It also includes an encounter with the emerging oral tradition of the first-century church. While it would be many decades—indeed centuries—before Paul's letters and the other New Testament writings would attain the full status of canonical scripture, the early postresurrection community began developing almost immediately an oral process of fashioning a christological worldview and perspective on the Jewish biblical material.[15] The apostle's use of scripture was not shaped only by his reading of the biblical texts, nor by Jewish traditions of interpretation, nor for that matter by his experience with Christ on the Damascus road. It was also apparently affected by the contour of this developing tradition of the early church.

As an interpreter of biblical material, Paul looked at the sacred text through the lens of Christ, a lens ground by both experience and tradition. But the apostle's religious and theological activity was not simply a private matter. Despite Paul's effort to minimize his reliance upon the Jerusalem apostles according to Galatians 1, it is still clear that he met with other apostles and followers of Christ. The accounts in Acts certainly confirm this (for example, Acts 15). While it may not be helpful to speculate about the nature of these conversations, it seems reasonable to conclude that Paul encountered the oral traditions of the early church through contacts with other apostles and followers of Jesus, as he went about the business of proclaiming the gospel. He was part of an emerging community, and he was affected by the emerging and sometimes amorphous traditions of that community. To be sure, Paul made his own contributions to these developing traditions, but what he heard and saw in scripture was formed by the interchange between a personal experience with Christ and the church's growing perception of how Christ was to be understood. Hence, when we speak of a conversation model of interpretation, we must acknowledge the fact that the mutually informing encounter between Paul and his biblical text was carried out against the backdrop of the early church's developing tradition.

Once again, the irony of all this is that the only way we have access to this oral tradition of the early church is through the church's literary legacy. Most of Paul's theological work undoubtedly had its inception in the act of orally proclaiming the gospel and debating the issues of concern to the Gentile churches. But we must also recognize that the question of orality extends to the issues of interpretive context and emerging tradition as well. The written texts of the New Testament will allow us to determine only in broad outline the form of these oral traditions. However, it is possible to focus this discussion by comparing biblical material common to Paul and other New Testament writers. In the case of Romans 9:33, we have the perspective of another interpreter of Jewish scripture, the writer of 1 Peter (2:6–8), against which to assess Paul's conversation with the biblical material and the developing tradition of the early church. And in Romans 10:16 and 15:21, we glimpse the way Paul has read and discerned the significance of the fourth "servant song" from Isaiah 52:13–53:12. These examples allow us to see that Paul's conversations with the Bible are taking place in the context of a larger series of biblical conversations that are going on among the early followers of Jesus. Paul may very well have been influenced by some of these other interpreters and interpretations but that can only be detected through careful investigation of individual texts.

Romans 9:33 and 1 Peter 2:6–8

The importance of this Pauline text in the development of early church tradition has been acknowledged and discussed repeatedly by biblical scholars.[16] This passage in Romans is significant for our purposes because both the apostle and the writer of 1 Peter reflect a combined quotation from Isaiah 28:16 and 8:14–15:

See, I am laying in Zion *a stone that will make people stumble, a rock that will make them fall,*
and whoever believes in him will not be put to shame. (Rom. 9:33)

A careful reading of Romans 9:33 shows that Isaiah 28:16 is the leading text into which Isaiah 8:14–15 has been incorporated. Moreover, it shows that the word "stone" (*lithos*) has functioned as the verbal link between the two prophetic verses.

In 1 Peter 2:6–8, however, the two prophetic references are linked together by Psalm 118:22. The textual similarities between Romans 9:33 and 1 Peter 2:6–8 are striking:

> "See, I am laying in Zion a stone,
>   a cornerstone chosen and precious;
> and whoever believes in him will not be put to shame."

To you then who believe, he is precious; but for those who do not believe,

> *"The stone that the builders rejected*
>   *has become the very head of the corner,"*

and

> "A stone that makes them stumble,
>   and a rock that makes them fall."   (1 Peter 2:6–8)

The fact that Psalm 118:22 has been included in the text of Peter, as well as the fact that the writer of 1 Peter has not reproduced exactly the combined quotation of Isaiah 28:16 and 8:14 as it appears in Romans 9:33, suggests that this textual similarity cannot be attributed to the literary dependence of 1 Peter on Romans. The more likely explanation is that there was a tradition in the early church in which these passages were combined and that this common tradition is reflected in both Romans and 1 Peter.[17] The precise form of this tradition cannot be determined perhaps, but the textual similarities between the two epistles point in the direction of either a written source or a stable oral tradition.

In 1 Peter, the citations are used in an exhortative context. The writer invites readers to come to the "living stone" that has been rejected but is chosen and precious in the sight of God. The writer exhorts readers, as "living stones," to be built into a spiritual house, to be a holy priesthood, and to bring spiritual sacrifices acceptable to God through Jesus Christ. Following this hortatory introduction, Isaiah 28:16 is quoted. From the context, it is evident that the "stone" is to be understood as Christ; but it is also obvious that the writer calls upon readers as "living stones" to be built into a spiritual house. In this text, the citation from Psalm 118:22 relates to the attitude toward the "stone" that is shared by those who believe, whereas the quotation from Isaiah 8:14 corresponds to what happens to those who do not believe. In 2:8b the writer of 1 Peter states: "They stumble because they disobey the word, as they were destined to do." For those who believe, however, the "stone" is precious. The "stone" is Christ and the readers are exhorted to come to Christ.

This discussion of 1 Peter 2:4–8 indicates that, although there is a difference between "believers" and "unbelievers" and their attitudes toward the "stone," the distinction between "works" and "faith" is not at issue as it is in Romans 9:30–33. Unlike Paul, the writer of 1 Peter calls upon readers to put off all manner of wickedness and to come to the Lord (1 Peter 1:13–2:10). The writer is concerned with holiness but not with two different ways of pursuing righteousness. In Romans, however, the scriptural quotations are used in a context that concerns the relationship between Jews and Gentiles. According to Paul, Israel has pursued righteousness in the wrong way. It has sought righteousness by "works" and not "faith." For Israel, Christ has become a stumbling block. And for the writer of 1 Peter, the stumbling occurs because of "unbelief" and disobedience, whereas for Paul it is largely the result of pursuing the law and righteousness in the wrong way.[18] In Romans 10:2, Paul concedes that the Jews have zeal for God, but it is not according to "knowledge." Because the "unbelieving" Jews have misunderstood the law and Christ, says Paul, they have stumbled.

Although Paul and the writer of 1 Peter have used Isaiah 28:16 and 8:14 in a manner that indicates that they share a common christological tradition, it is clear that the authors have understood the scriptural material in quite different ways. It is also apparent that neither these texts nor this early christological tradition restrained the apostle Paul from using the biblical material to his own advantage. On the contrary, the manner in which Paul has inserted Isaiah 28:16 and 8:14 into the discussion in Romans 9:30–33 strongly suggests that Paul has placed this early Christian interpretive tradition in the service of a specific message ("works" versus "faith") which he seeks to communicate to the followers of Christ in Rome.

It has been argued that the term "stone" in Romans 9:33 refers primarily to Torah and not to Christ.[19] Israel mistakenly pursued the law by "works" instead of by "faith" and because of that stumbled.

Nevertheless, it is recognized that there cannot be an unqualified connection between the "stone" and Torah in 9:33, because the pronoun "him" ("Whoever believes in *him* will not be put to shame") from Isaiah 28:16 (also cited in Rom. 10:11) almost certainly refers to Christ in both 9:33 and 10:11.[20] While there is a close connection between Christ and Torah in Romans 10:1–8, the most probable interpretation is that Christ is the referent of both the "stone" and the pronoun "him" in 9:33 and 10:11.

Hence, Paul reflects the connection found elsewhere in the New Testament between Christ and the "stone" (see Matt. 21:42, Mark 12:10, Luke 20:17–18, Acts 4:11). It is not a matter of imposing the views of other New Testament authors on Paul to suggest that he has used the popular association in early church tradition between Christ and the "stone" but has done so in order to address a specific Pauline issue, in particular the way righteousness is to be obtained. In fact, the textual and thematic characteristics of Romans 9:30–33 suggest that the apostle has been drawn to the christological view of the scriptural material through his familiarity with the traditions of the emerging apostolic community and at same time has refashioned his understanding of the material to suit his own purposes. In this case, the interaction between the biblical text and the interpretive context includes the developing christological tradition of the church. In one sense, Paul's dialogue with the verses from Isaiah begins not with the prophetic texts themselves but with the way the texts have come to be read and understood in the early church. The apostle is not constrained by this developing tradition, but, as nearly as we can tell, he has constructed from this tradition a discussion about "works" and "faith," law and righteousness.

Romans 10:16 and 15:21

Isaiah 52:13–53:12 (the fourth "servant song") is a block of scriptural material from which Paul quotes twice in Romans. In Romans 10:16, the statement is made that "not all have obeyed the good news." This assertion is followed by a citation from Isaiah 53:1:

"Lord, who has believed our message?" The literary context of this quotation in Romans indicates that the verse has been applied to the response of the Jews to apostolic preaching. The passage has not been applied directly to Christ. The second Pauline citation from this block of scriptural material is Isaiah 52:15 found in Romans 15:21. This biblical reference follows Paul's statement:

> Thus, I make it my ambition to proclaim the good news, not where Christ has already been named, so that I do not build on someone else's foundation, but as it is written,
>
> > "Those who have never been told of him shall see,
> >   and those who have never heard of him shall understand."

Although the pronoun "him" must be a reference to Christ, the context of this quotation indicates that the main theme of this discussion, as in Romans 10:16, concerns preaching.

Though only one of these two passages is quoted elsewhere in the New Testament (Isa. 53:1 in John 12:38), it is instructive to note the way the Gospel writers have used citations from the rest of the fourth "servant song." In Matthew 8:17, a quotation from Isaiah 53:4 has been inserted into an account in which Jesus is portrayed as a man who heals the sick and exorcises demons. Matthew writes: "This was to fulfill what had been spoken through the prophet Isaiah, 'He took our infirmities and bore our diseases.' " The evangelist has identified Jesus the healer and exorcist with the figure of the servant by announcing that in Jesus of Nazareth the word of the prophet Isaiah has been fulfilled.

In his account of the Last Supper, Luke also quotes from this section of scripture (Isa. 53:12 in Luke 22:37). As in Matthew 8:17, the citation is introduced with a formula in which Jesus is portrayed as fulfilling or completing the words of scripture. Luke writes: "For I tell you, this scripture must be fulfilled [completed] in me, 'And he was counted among the lawless'; and indeed what is written about me is being fulfilled [completed]." In Luke, the introduction and the citation are spoken by Jesus, but in Matthew the formula and the quotation are editorial comments. Yet in both Gospel texts the scriptural references have been linked directly to Jesus. Luke again quotes from this block of material (Isa. 53:7–8) in Acts 8:32–33 as part of the story of the Ethiopian eunuch. Following the citation that is depicted as being read by the eunuch, Luke writes: "The eunuch asked Philip, 'About whom, may I ask you, does the prophet say this, about himself or about someone else?' Then Philip began to speak, and starting with this scripture, he proclaimed to him the good news about Jesus" (Acts 8:34–35). Once again, it is clear that Luke intends this saying in Isaiah 53:7–8 to apply directly to Jesus. He is the servant.[21]

John is the only New Testament writer other than Paul to quote Isaiah 53:1 (12:38). John writes:

> Although he had performed so many signs in their presence, they did not believe him. This was to fulfill the word spoken by the prophet Isaiah:
>
> "Lord, who has believed our message,
>   and to whom has the arm of the Lord been revealed?"
>
> (John 12:37–38)

As in the Synoptic Gospels, the material from Isaiah is introduced as being fulfilled, but its fulfillment, according to John, is in the fact that Jesus' signs have not been believed because it was necessary that scripture be fulfilled. Both John and Paul have used Isaiah 53:1 in relation to "unbelief," but in the Gospel "unbelief" is a response to Jesus' signs, whereas in Romans 10:16 it is a response to apostolic preaching.

As we have already noted, both of the passages cited by Paul are used in contexts that pertain to preaching. In Romans 10:14–16 Paul claims that there is a connection between "belief" and the sending of preachers. Although preachers have been sent, not all have believed. As in John 12:38, Isaiah 53:1 is used by Paul in connection with "unbelief." For Paul, however, "unbelief" is not portrayed as a response to Jesus' signs. There is little question that the figure of Christ was central in Paul's understanding of missionary preaching, but it is evident that this scriptural citation is understood by him as relating to the Christ of apostolic proclamation and not specifically to the life and ministry of Jesus. It might be argued that this distinction is due to the difference between an epistle and a Gospel as forms of literature. While this is undoubtedly a factor to be considered, it appears that the distinction is more substantial than this. For Paul, Christ is represented in the act of proclamation.

In Romans 15:17–21, the apostle writes about his ministry among the Gentiles. He claims that it has been his ambition to preach the gospel where Christ has not yet been named so that he might not build on the work of another. As a way of illustrating this, he cites Isaiah 52:15. The point of Paul's discussion is to show, with the aid of scripture, that he has desired to proclaim the gospel to those who have never heard about Christ. In this example, too, Paul understands the scriptural passage as relating to the Christ of apostolic proclamation. This illustrates that, although Paul's selection and use of the Isaiah texts has come within the pale of the early church's identification of the servant of Isaiah with Christ, he has used the two verses in conformity with his own conception of Christology, preaching, and the Gentile mission.

Conclusion

The biblical text as sacred scripture in many ways epitomizes the literary substance of the Christian community's religious system. In letter and in thematic development, the text of the Bible provides a line of continuity from one generation to the next, as the community practices its religion and reflects upon its system of beliefs. By definition, scripture holds a position of authority in a religious community. From that point of view, it supplies an arena within which religious and theological thinking take place. For Paul, the Jew, the scriptural texts of his people also served this function. They provided a source of stimulation for his religious imagination, served as an object of reflection, and functioned as a place within which to discern the workings of God.

Yet, as we have seen, the meaning of the biblical text does not present itself to Paul as something that is self-evident or readily accessible by itself. In fact, Paul engages the biblical text in the epistles as an apostle and as a follower of Christ. Through the Spirit and from the point of view of having come to understand the hidden purposes of God in Christ, the apostle encounters the "world" of the biblical text. It is in the merging of the "world" of the text and the "world" of Paul's apostolic context that the biblical material begins to take on new meaning for the apostle. New ways of understanding biblical texts begin to emerge. And new ways of construing the purposes of God for the redemption of the world start to take shape in Paul's encounter with his Bible. But Paul's use of the Bible is not an abstract or detached kind of endeavor. It is grounded in the missionary work of this first-century evangelist. It is grounded in an interaction in which Paul engages the biblical text and out of which emerges a framework of theological meaning. In short, the apostle was involved in shifting structures of religious meaning, and the biblical text served as one of the agents in that process. While there is, as we have seen, continuity between Paul and his Jewish religious heritage, there is also discontinuity as the apostle pushes his religious worldview to the edge, and perhaps beyond, the pale of first-century Jewish religion and theology.

The final element in Paul's hermeneutic is his audience, the people to whom he directs his preaching and his writing. To the extent that we know anything in detail about these people, we find out most directly through the letters that Paul has written to them. It is not our purpose to debate issues of Pauline readership, but it is important to be reminded again that the apostle as a preacher and as a writer of epistles is engaged in a process of communication. He not only seeks to inform his audience about certain theological and pastoral matters but strives to maintain unity in the church and to conform his readers' behavior to his own vision of the gospel. Paul does hermeneutics and theology primarily for the sake of his mission to the Gentiles and for the people who are encountered along the way.

If we look closely at the argument so far, we can see that at least five elements are involved in Paul's conversation with the Bible: (1) the biblical text, (2) his apostolic and christological context, (3) the developing christological traditions of the early church, (4) the developing traditions of early Judaism, and (5) the readers (or hearers) of his epistles. All of these play a role in the apostle's encounter with biblical material.

Paul's explicit biblical quotations and the manner of their incorporation into his epistles, as displayed in this chapter, indicate that the biblical text as a literary text is important for the way Paul structures many of his arguments. The *text* of scripture is a conversation partner for Paul. Chapter II has also made it abundantly clear that Paul's interpretive voice has been shaped by his apostolic and christological circumstance. Christ crucified and risen is Paul's prime point of reference for entering into dialogue with scripture. At the same time, we have now seen that the early church's emergent christological tradition was capable of influencing, if not shaping, Paul's perception of a given biblical text. This christological tradition did not, of course, constrain him from bringing the scriptural text into conformity with his own immediate argument. Furthermore, Paul read scripture theologically and apocalyptically as a Jew. Jewish traditions and categories of thought gave Paul a context for understanding the church, Christology, and his own work among the Gentiles. Out of this matrix, Paul sought to communicate with readers in Galatia, Rome, and elsewhere. He addressed the pressing problems of the churches in Gentile lands and sought to preserve their unity in the face of division and schism.

In the next four chapters, we shall examine four specific Pauline conversations with scripture. We shall look at the way in which the voice of Paul and the voice of scripture come together to form a series of individual conversations. The focal points for these conversations are Abraham, Israel, Adam, and Torah/wisdom. In the chapters that follow, we shall lend our ear to these dialogues between Paul and scripture.

Paul's Conversation with Scripture

IV

Abraham and the Gospel of Inclusion

In Galatians 3:16, Paul identifies Christ as the offspring of Abraham. The apostle makes a direct link between the promise given to the patriarch and the fulfillment of that promise in the birth of Jesus Christ. Virtually any Jew in the first century would have known that Isaac was the fulfillment of the promise made to Abraham and would have been perplexed, probably offended, by the suggestion that Christ somehow epitomized the completion of God's word to the patriarch. Although Paul does not explicitly use the language of promise and fulfillment in the development of his Christology,[1] it is clearly implied in the identification of Christ with the seed of Abraham.[2] According to Paul, that which has been promised to Abraham has now been brought to fulfillment in Jesus Christ.

Paul's focus on the singular form of the word "seed" (*sperma*) certainly strains the intended meaning of the biblical text. Then as now, the collective singular of the words "seed" or "offspring" could be used to mean more than one person. In fact, the people of Israel as a whole were the offspring of Abraham through Isaac and Jacob. Yet, Paul's technique of interpretation in Galatians 3:16 is grounded in a basic Jewish presupposition: scripture is meaningful in all its parts. Accordingly, if the word "seed" appears in the singular form, this may imply something specific about the meaning of the biblical text. In this case, Paul has sought to link the singular form of the word "seed" with the one person who stands at the center of his religious worldview.

73

Hence, Paul is asserting that Christ is the son of Abraham in a unique sense. He is not the offspring of Abraham simply by virtue of his Jewishness but because he is the Christ. This is not a self-evident claim, and it is not a claim that would have made sense to the vast majority of Jews in Paul's day. But it is an assertion that enables the apostle to establish a connection between Christ and the promise that was made to the patriarch. Furthermore, this connection allows the apostle to identify those who are "in Christ" (and therefore descendants of Abraham) with the people of God (Gal. 3:26–29). In the economy of redemption, this signifies a structural link based on the promise and fulfillment of God (compare 2 Sam. 7:12–14).

This claim, of course, involves a redefinition of the historic people of the covenant and would have been offensive to those Jews who did not share Paul's conviction that Jesus was the promised Messiah. To compound the problem, Paul was arguing that Gentiles could be included among the people of God without first being circumcised and declaring their adherence to the law of Moses. Not only would this have threatened the integrity of Judaism as a religious community, but more importantly it would have strained the social relationships between those who followed Christ and agreed with Paul and those who did not agree with him. In other words, Paul's identification of Christ as the offspring of Abraham and the followers of Christ as people of God was of more than theoretical interest. The message of the apostle was bound to have been disquieting and divisive, for it challenged the historic definitions of what it meant to be a Jew. This was to have important consequences for Paul and for the relationship between the church and the synagogue.

In terms of Paul's conversation with the Genesis narrative, the meaning of the Abrahamic covenant has clearly been transformed. Implicit in Paul's argument is the conviction that he knows what constitutes the fulfillment of the divine word. Thus, Paul approaches the biblical promise from the perspective of its fulfillment. Paul is convinced that Christ is the fulfillment of God's intention for the salvation of humankind. With that christological presupposition in mind, he can assert that God's word to Abraham is in effect the promise to which Christ is the fulfillment. The promise to Abraham points forward to Christ, argues Paul. But that prospective viewpoint is shaped by the belief that Christ is the redeemer of the world. The promise to Abraham gives Paul another conceptual framework from which to view the identity of Christ, as well as the identity of the people of God. The scriptural narrative, as well as Jewish tradition, transmits the promise, and the Christ-centered conviction of the early church embodies its fulfillment. In the apostle, the Jew and follower of Christ, the two come together to undergird the Gentile mission.

At the heart of Paul's reflection on the Abrahamic material is a concern for the inclusion of Gentiles into the community of Christ. This is what drives Paul's understanding of Abraham. His primary concern is not personal salvation or a private relationship with God. Paul's interest is corporate. It has to do with the community of Christ and the way a person becomes part of that community. It is by faith and not works that Gentiles enter into the fellowship of Christ and become part of his body. This is Paul's gospel of inclusion. Those on the outside, the Gentiles, through faith are made members of the body of Christ. This is an important message that Paul offers Christian communities today. In a time when there is increasing concern for inclusiveness, Paul reminds us of the corporate character of the gospel. Today, the issue for the church is not the inclusion of Gentiles into a largely Jewish community of Christ, but the inclusion of all sorts of people who have been excluded, for whatever reason, from participation in the fellowship of Christ. To be sure, Paul's concern was not marginalized people in general. He had a specific Jew/Gentile concern in mind. But it is certainly legitimate for modern interpreters of Paul to focus on the corporate and inclusive character of the Pauline gospel and to build on that feature of Paul's theology rather than focus on the personal nature of faith righteousness, as has been done in Western Christianity since the time of Augustine. The rediscovery of Paul's gospel of inclusion is vitally important, and his reinterpretation of the Abrahamic material is the place to begin.

The Lord Reckoned It to Him as Righteousness

With the call of Abraham in Genesis 12, the legend of Israel's origin begins. This is one of the constitutive legends of Israel, and it

establishes the genealogical identity of the people of God. At the heart of
this story stand two basic elements: (1) the predicament of Abraham and
Sarah and (2) the promise of God. God promises Abraham that God will
bless him and make his name great. As the narrative proceeds, it
becomes clear to the reader that this promise means that Abraham will
have an heir (and many descendants) and that these descendants will be
given a land to call their own. In the fulfillment of these promises,
Abraham will be blessed and his name will be great among the nations of
the earth. Abraham and his descendants will be the recipients of the
blessing of God, but they, too, will be the agent of blessing. "I will bless
those who bless you, and the one who curses you I will curse; and in you
all the families of the earth shall be blessed" (Gen. 12:3).

Against the background of this promise, the predicament that drives
the narrative stands in sharp contrast. Abraham is an old man, and
Sarah, his wife, is well beyond childbearing years. The circumstance of
the principal characters in the story seems to collide with the word of
God. How can God's promise be fulfilled under these circumstances?
According to custom in the ancient Near East, it was acceptable to devise
a surrogate mother arrangement as a way of dealing with the problem of
childlessness.[3] This is precisely what Sarah proposes to Abraham.
Hagar, Sarah's maid, is given to Abraham in order that she might give
birth to his heir. Indeed she does conceive and Ishmael is born. Even
though Ishmael is born as Abraham's son, he is not to be the child of
promise. It is announced that Ishmael will be made a great nation, but
Sarah will be the mother of Abraham's heir, the child of promise.

In Genesis 15:1–6, the reader is presented with a dialogue between
God and Abraham. Having been told not to fear, Abraham questions
God: "O Lord God, what will you give me, for I continue childless, and
the heir of my house is Eliezer of Damascus [a person not identified
further]? . . . 'You have given me no offspring, and so a slave born in my
house is to be my heir.' " In response to Abraham's anguished cry, the
promise of numerous descendants is made. Eliezer is not to be
Abraham's heir, and his offspring will be as many as the stars in the
heavens. To this promise, the reader is told that Abraham responded by
believing the words that God had spoken to him. The episode concludes
in 15:6 with a terse announcement: "And he believed the Lord; and the

Lord reckoned it to him as righteousness." Despite the vicissitudes of the story line, the reader is presented with the picture of a man who trusts and believes the promise of God and is therefore reckoned to be righteous or just.

In the text of Genesis 15:6, three words appear that prove to be instrumental for Paul in the use of this biblical passage: (1) the verb "to believe," (2) the verb "to reckon," and (3) the noun "righteousness." Relying on the Greek version of Genesis, as Paul undoubtedly did, enables him to use the Greek forms of these words to generate the familiar notion of "justification by faith." The text of Genesis 15:6 as it stands in the narrative of Sarah and Abraham most certainly does not have to do directly with the Pauline idea of "justification by faith," but the passage presents Paul with a theological image and a series of words that he is able to mold into the concept that we have come to know as "justification by faith." The Greek verb that means "to believe" is, of course, a cognate of the Greek word that is translated "faith" in English; and the Greek word that is rendered "righteousness" is indirectly related to our English word "justification." Since there is no English equivalent of the Greek verb that would normally be translated "to righteous," we generally use the word "justify" instead.[4] On a technical level, these words enable Paul to generate a concept of righteousness based on faith (in Christ), even though the text of scripture itself is apparently about something quite different. It suffices to say at this point that Genesis 15:6 provided the verbal grist for the apostle's attempt to deal with the issue of the Gentiles and their relationship to the promises of God. By using these key words, Paul was able to formulate a distinctive way of understanding God's relationship with the Jews, as well as his inclusion of the Gentiles among the chosen people.

The issue for us here is not simply whether Paul was right or wrong in his interpretation of the Genesis material. Rather, it is a question of the way in which the apostle has construed the meaning of the biblical story in order to generate a theological discussion. In this regard, the statement, "And he believed the Lord and the Lord reckoned it to him as righteousness," is seen to be the pivotal component in Paul's use of the Sarah/Abraham narrative. It is this central component that the apostle elaborates in order to undergird his mission to the Gentiles. In view of the problems encountered in the Gentile mission, Paul searched the Genesis material for a way of understanding the relationship between the Jews and the Gentiles. In the process, the scriptural text provided the apostle with a set of concepts that he discovered could be applied to the issues facing him. Paul searched the biblical text, and the biblical text in turn addressed him. The result was a creative theological response to the issue at hand. Though Paul presumably thought he had uncovered the "true" meaning of the Genesis text, the end product was certainly in the realm of religious and theological argumentation rather than historical-critical interpretation. In other words, the apostle was using the text to address a specific religious issue and was not seeking the meaning of the historical text for its own sake.

The story of Sarah and Abraham is more than an interesting tale. It functioned as one of Israel's national legends, and it established the nation of Israel as the people of promise. Tracing their descent through Jacob and Isaac to Abraham, the Jews could literally view themselves as a living expression of the fulfillment of God's promise to Abraham. Through Isaac, the promise had been passed on to Jacob and to the nation of Israel. As the people looked into their past, they could identify themselves as the promised, indeed chosen, people. They could see who they were and who they were not. They were the descendants of Abraham. They were not the offspring of Ishmael or Esau.

It may have been that the story of Sarah and Abraham itself emerged in part as an attempt to explain how the people of Yahweh came into being. After the fact, the people of Israel shaped and elaborated the stories of the ancient past to fit and explain the present reality of the nation. In the process, the identity of the community was established and perpetuated. Each new generation was incorporated into the community's "myth" of self-identification. The promise to Abraham was seen to have been fulfilled by the fact of Israel's very existence.

Paul, the Jew, certainly was familiar with this story, and he undoubtedly had been impressed by the promissory character of the narrative. But Paul had also come to believe that Jesus was the Messiah. Furthermore, he had come to believe passionately that the Gentiles were under no obligation to adhere to the requirement of circumcision. As we shall see, the claim that non-Jews could be included among the people of promise without becoming proselytes transformed the accepted meaning of the Sarah/Abraham story. The apostle sought to maintain the identity-enhancing function of the story while placing it in the service of a new definition of the people of God. Not only did Paul perceive Christ to be the offspring of Abraham, but he understood all those who are "in Christ" to be descendants of the patriarch as well (Gal. 3:26–29). The promise to Abraham became a tool that the apostle sought to use in order to establish the identity of the church. Even more than a tool, however, the story of Sarah and Abraham provided a scriptural framework for understanding the church's place in the plan of God.

The Genesis account of Sarah and Abraham does not function preeminently to establish the identity of individuals but to establish the identity of a community, of which the people of Israel as individuals are a part. In applying this biblical material to the circumstance of the Gentiles, Paul has maintained the corporate implication of the text and has pointed to "faith" as the means whereby Gentiles are included in the community of the righteous. Through an encounter with the text of Genesis, Paul has developed a vocabulary to describe the transfer of Gentiles from being "outsiders" to being "insiders." For the modern church, it is at this point that Paul's use of Abraham is instructive. The Abrahamic stories in Genesis, and Paul's use of them in the epistles, do not focus on personal sin and forgiveness. They have to do with identity, and Paul uses them to describe the way a person comes to be identified with a particular community, the community of Christ. Through dialogue with the story of Abraham, Paul reinterprets the meaning of Genesis. Indeed, he extends the meaning of the narrative well beyond its historical roots, and in so doing he gives us a clue about the extension and application of those texts in the modern Christian context. Paul suggests that inclusion, the manner of one's inclusion, and identity are at stake for the church and its proclamation. The apostle's gospel of inclusion ought not, it seems, be reduced to a message of individual righteousness and personal salvation.

The Righteous Will Live by Faith

The earliest reference to Genesis 15:6 in the extant letters of Paul is Galatians 3:6. Following a statement of undisguised exasperation at the beginning of chapter 3, the apostle embarks on an attempt to show that "works" are opposed to "faith." In the biblical exposition that opens in Galatians 3:6, Genesis 15:6 is the leading scriptural text. It is quoted by Paul, and it sets the stage for the discussion that follows. In fact, immediately following the scriptural citation, the apostle appends his interpretation of the passage. He writes: ". . . so, you see, those who believe are the descendants of Abraham." By focusing on the faith of the patriarch, Paul has concluded that the descendants of Abraham are in fact the people of faith (in Christ). To historical-critical eyes, this conclusion certainly skews the meaning of Genesis 15:6. However, Paul is not finished. He continues: "And the scripture, foreseeing that God would justify the Gentiles by faith, declared the gospel beforehand to Abraham, saying, 'All the Gentiles shall be blessed in you' " (Gal. 3:8).[5] The Greek word *ethnē* can be translated either as "nations" or "Gentiles." But it is clear that Paul has used the word *ethnē* here to refer to the Gentile mission. The apostle considers God's promise to Abraham to be an announcement authorizing the inclusion of Gentiles into the community on the basis of faith and not obedience to Torah. Those who have faith in Christ share the blessing that was pronounced upon Abraham. Indeed they, themselves, bring to completion that which God announced to the patriarch because they represent the fulfillment of God's word.

The apostle's discussion in Galatians 3:6–9 is not an abstract treatise on the issue of "faith" versus "works." Paul is engaged in a debate with those who challenged his claims about the law of Moses and the necessity of circumcision.[6] This situation has given birth to the discussion, and it is this situation that provides the debate with its historical context. Paul is responding to charges that have been leveled against him. His authority as an apostle has been challenged. For our purposes, it is not necessary to determine the precise nature of this conflict. But it is important to keep in mind that Paul is writing to a community that claims to follow Christ, a community made up of both

Jews and Gentiles. As the founder of the Galatian churches, the apostle is writing to straighten out the problems that have erupted and to keep the community from falling apart. Hence, this interpretation of biblical texts is part of an "in-house" discussion.

In that light, we can see that Paul is responding to a situation that presupposes the existence of a community held together by its messianic conviction. By the time the epistle is written, the church in Galatia forms an established community. Thus, Paul's use of material from the Sarah/Abraham narrative serves not only to establish "faith" as the basis for receiving the blessing of Abraham but also to identify the people who believe in Christ as the descendants of the patriarch. The argument is designed to distinguish between "faith" and "works," but in the process the biblical texts are used to argue that the church represents the offspring of Abraham. By basing the church's identity on faith in Christ instead of Torah, the apostle is also able to redefine who the people of Abraham are. This redefinition would certainly have been considered outside the "circle of plausibility" for the overwhelming majority of Jews, but internally within the church it could be used to justify the inclusion of Gentiles among the people of God. Even within the church, however, the apostle's argument was controversial and was not accepted by everyone. Paul's use of Abraham as an exemplary figure is provocative for a number of reasons, not least of which is the redefinition of the people of God. If the Jewish community was to continue as it had been defined historically, the claims of Paul clearly had to be rejected.

The twin issues of the law and the identity of the people of God are addressed by Paul in Galatians 3:15–29 (4:1–7) and 4:21–31. If the law of Moses is not obligatory for inclusion among the people of God, the apostle understands that he then is compelled to address what he considers to be the real purpose of the law. First, he seeks to establish that the law of Moses in no way countermands the promise that God gave to Abraham. He writes: "I give an example from daily life: once a person's will has been ratified, no one adds to it or annuls it. . . . the law, which came four hundred thirty years later, does not annul a covenant previously ratified by God, so as to nullify the promise" (Gal. 3:15,17). Although Moses received the law well after the covenant with Abraham, the apostle argues that God's promise has not been set aside. God's relationship with Abraham's descendants is still based on the promise that was made long ago.

In itself this claim may not have raised any significant objections. But neither does it address the heart of the issue. It simply prepares the way for the second part of Paul's discussion, in which he attempts to account for the giving of the law. "Why then the law? It was added because of transgressions, until the offspring would come to whom the promise had been made" (Gal. 3:19). Whether this passage means that the law was given to bring transgressions to life or to curb transgressions is a matter of debate.[7] In either case, however, it is clear that Paul thought the law's validity was to be of limited duration. Moreover, it is repeated once again that the law is not against the promises of God. With the familiar *mē genoito* ("by no means"), Paul emphatically denies that the law is contrary to God's promise. Until the coming of Christ, the law was to function as a tutor or disciplinarian (*paidagōgos*). "Now before faith came, we were imprisoned and guarded under the law until faith would be revealed. Therefore the law was our disciplinarian until Christ came, so that we might be justified by faith" (Gal. 3:23–24). At the beginning of chapter 4, Paul elaborates this point. He likens the circumstance of the law to an heir who, though the inheritor of the estate, is under a guardian until the time appointed by the father. The law of Moses was given to serve this custodial function until the coming of Christ.

In seeking to identify the function of the law, the apostle views Christ as pivotal. As Paul writes in Galatians 3:14: ". . . in order that in Christ Jesus the blessing of Abraham might come to the Gentiles, so that we might receive the promise of the Spirit through faith." The law is not against the promises of God, but its usefulness has come to an end. In Christ, the blessing of Abraham has come to the Gentiles, and they have been made heirs of God's promise. Except for the direct references to Christ in Galatians 3:13 and 16, it is evident that Paul has not used explicit scriptural citations to elaborate his christological conviction. But it is equally clear that the apostle has brought his messianic conviction to bear on his reassessment of the law and has sought to overlay the figure of Abraham with christological imagery.

In turn, the biblical echoes and images are used as a framework for fashioning a quite novel understanding of the law. They are also used to forge a redefinition of the people of God.

Unwilling to terminate the debate with his opponents, Paul challenges them once again. In the so-called Sarah/Hagar allegory (Gal. 4:21–31), the apostle questions: "Tell me, you who desire to be subject to the law, will you not *listen to* [my emphasis] the law?" Ostensibly the argument is about the law of Moses. And in a play on the meaning of the word "law," the apostle challenges those who claim the necessity of obedience to the Mosaic law by directing them to the Pentateuch, in order to show them what the biblical law says. Without hesitation the apostle turns again to the story of Sarah and Abraham. On this occasion, however, Paul focuses on the women in the narrative, Sarah and her maid Hagar. For Paul, the women represent two groups of people, as expressed in two lines of descent.

Sarah (free woman)	*Hagar (slave woman)*
Son of promise	Son of Flesh
	Mount Sinai
	Bears children for slavery
Jerusalem above	Present Jerusalem
Our free mother	In slavery with her children

With an eye on maternal descent, Paul focuses on the freedom of Sarah and the slavery of Hagar. The key concepts of freedom and slavery become, in the apostle's argument, the basis for distinguishing two groups of people. Those free people who are born according to the promise of God are separated from those enslaved people who are born according to the arrangement with Hagar. Virtually all Jews would have understood themselves as standing in the line of Sarah. The Jews, after all, were the people of promise. They were the heirs of God's covenant with Abraham and Sarah. Paul, however, turns the genealogy around. He argues that the people of promise are the followers of Christ when he writes: "Now you [we?], my friends, are children of the promise, like Isaac" (Gal. 4:28). For the apostle, it is not the Torah-observant Jew who is the child of promise. It is the follower of Christ set free from the law of Moses who lays claim to being called the descendant of Abraham.

In a dramatic, some may say perverse, turnabout of the Sarah/ Abraham story, Paul has sought to establish the people of God on a new and different foundation. According to Paul, Jews are certainly to be included among the people of God, but so are Gentiles. Yet the basis upon which both Jews and Gentiles are to be included among the people of God is faith in Christ and not physical descent from Abraham and Sarah or obedience to the law of Moses.

Furthermore, Paul is adamant about not confusing the distinction between the two ways of identifying the people of God. He writes: "But just as at that time the child who was born according to the flesh persecuted the child who was born according to the Spirit, so it is now also. But what does the scripture *say* [my emphasis]? 'Drive out the slave and her child; for the child of the slave will not share the inheritance with the child of the free woman' " (Gal. 4:29–30, quoting Gen. 21:10). The apostle argues that there is no middle ground. Moreover, faith and promise are the key factors in identifying the "true" progeny of the patriarch/matriarch. However, faith and promise are not without specific content. For Paul, faith is faith in Christ and the promise is the promise that Christ is to be the fulfillment of God's word to Abraham. Thus, the entire conversation in Galatians 4:21–31 is predicated on a christological foundation.

In light of the way Paul has listened to and encountered the biblical story, it is clear that he has used the concepts of the scriptural text but given them new content. Furthermore, he has maintained one of the primary functions of the biblical text: namely, to establish identity. The apostle has used the concept of faith and sought to argue that circumcision and law are not requirements for salvation. He has also used the concept of promise to connect the church with the historical claims of the people of Israel.

There is no question that Paul has turned the accepted meaning of the biblical narrative on its head. That is what makes Paul controversial. But it is equally evident that the apostle has not simply turned away from the biblical traditions of his people. Neither has he been able to dissociate himself from the concepts and categories that were part of his religious heritage. On the contrary, the apostle has sought to use them in order that they might inform the way in which the church operates and understands itself in relation to the Gentile world. The interaction between Paul and the Genesis narrative has produced a discussion in which Christology and biblical interpretation intersect. Paul has not simply repeated the accepted meaning of the biblical narrative, but neither has he ravaged the text with absolute disregard for its function.

The second reference to Genesis 15:6 is in Romans 4:3. This citation ought to be seen in light of Paul's broader concern for divine righteousness. In Romans 1:17, for example, the apostle writes: "For in it the righteousness of God is revealed through faith for faith; as it is written, 'The one who is righteous will live by faith.' " As the context indicates, Paul is also concerned to show that the salvation of God is available to everyone who has faith, both the Jew and the Greek. Hence, the citation from Habakkuk 2:4 is used to confirm the proposition that faith is the basis of salvation. This discussion is not taken up directly again until chapter 4, where Paul focuses once more on the key words "to believe," "to reckon," and "righteousness" from Genesis 15:6.

In Romans 4, the apostle engages in a sustained discussion of righteousness by faith. Much of what is contained in this argument has already been discussed in connection with Galatians and need not be rehearsed again, but several features must be noted. In Romans 4:3–5, the apostle makes explicit his distinction between a wage and a gift. Abraham believed God, and he was reckoned as righteous. He did nothing to earn God's favor. He was not declared righteous because of his lawful obedience. Furthermore, Paul connects Genesis 15:6 with Psalm 32:1–2. This link probably has not come about because of some underlying thematic connection between the two passages. Rather, the apostle has used the Jewish technique of claiming a connection between two passages in which a common word appears.[8] In this case, the word that appears in both is the verb "to reckon." According to this

technique of interpretation, both Genesis 15:6 and Psalm 32:1–2
contain the verb "to reckon"; therefore that which pertains in the case
of one passage obtains also in the case of the other. Thus, it is evident
that the apostle has seen the link between the Psalm and the Genesis
narrative to be based on the idea of "reckoning."

Another aspect of Romans 4 that must be addressed is the matter of
Abraham's circumcision. Paul asks the question: "We say, 'Faith was
reckoned to Abraham as righteousness.' How then was it reckoned to
him? Was it before or after he had been circumcised?" In answer to his
own question, he writes: "It was not after, but before he was
circumcised. He received the sign of circumcision as a seal of the
righteousness that he had by faith while he was still uncircumcised"
(4:9–11). In short, this observation is based on the fact that in the
narrative Abraham is reckoned as being righteous in Genesis 15:6, but
not until Genesis 17 is it stated that he was circumcised. By implication,
it might be concluded that the patriarch was reckoned as being
righteous apart from the requirement of circumcision. This technique
is also based on a Jewish method of interpretation that asserts that
literary sequence may be used as evidence of temporal chronology.
Therefore, circumcision was subsequent to faith. For Paul, this means
that circumcision is peripheral as far as the present-day community is
concerned. In turn, this is used as a way of establishing the argument
of righteousness by faith and distinguishing the gift of God from works
of law.

The historical context for Paul's use of the Genesis material
concerns the way in which the Gentiles are to be included among the
people of God and are to share his promises. Paul was not disenchanted with the religion of Israel. Neither was he filled with anxiety
born of the search for a merciful and gracious God.[9] But he was
convinced that he had been given the task of bringing the message of
Christ to the Gentiles. Moreover, the apostle came to believe that the
Gentiles did not need to assume the obligations of Torah. This was an
issue about which there were differences of opinion. It is also an issue
that generated great passion. For these reasons, Paul was compelled to
work out a way of understanding the salvation of the Gentiles. In the
the Sarah/Abraham narrative, the apostle discovered images and

concepts that he could exploit for the purpose of dealing with this issue and with his opponents.

Conclusion

Paul's letters have been applied by many different interpreters down through the history of the church to many different theological situations. We think, for example, of Martin Luther, John Calvin, and John Wesley. The issues that these individuals addressed were born of their own historical circumstances. They were not the same circumstances that prevailed in the first century. Those later interpreters used the letters to address their own peculiar situations. Later circumstances must not be confused with the historical context within which Paul used the Abrahamic material.[10] However, these later theologians and reformers had the right idea. The significance of the epistles is not limited to the first century, any more than the significance of Abraham was confined to the ancient history of the Pentateuchal period. This is a presupposition of the canon itself. The meaning and significance of the Bible extends beyond its historical period. It serves as a foundational document for an ongoing community, and its implications must continually be worked out in light of new circumstances. I am suggesting, moreover, that attention to Paul's interpretation of the Abrahamic material points the modern interpreter away from an individualistic understanding of the Pauline gospel and toward a recognition of its corporate character. It points away from notions of sin and guilt and toward the gospel's message of inclusion, a message that breaks down entrance requirements and removes barriers. It points away from privatistic religion and toward a community-based Christianity centered in faith.

Generalizations are always difficult in these matters, but it seems, by way of illustration, that the perception of the human predicament (sin) manifested among people in modern Western societies is not by and large a feeling of guilt before God or perhaps even a matter of meaninglessness. Some have described it rather as a sense of alienation—that is, alienation from self, others, community, and the earth itself. Modern, technologically advanced societies can very often separate people from a sense of their own identity, as well as isolate them from each other. Individualization comes to be isolation, and isolation comes to be separation. When this happens, people become disconnected from a sense of their own identity as people and lose a sense of their social character as human beings. The result is that people can end up being at odds with themselves, others, and the planet that sustains them.

To the extent that this description is accurate, the rediscovery that the Abrahamic stories speak about identity and that the Pauline gospel is about inclusion can begin to provide a biblical basis for addressing the problem of alienation. The gospel is corporate, not private. It is inclusive, not exclusive. It leads to identity, not to alienation. To develop a new appreciation for the context of the modern situation can lead to a renewed understanding of the Pauline gospel. And to arrive at a new perception of the way Paul uses the stories of Abraham and Sarah can in turn help us define anew the function of the gospel. We do not repristinate Paul and his setting, but we do extend the message of Paul into our own setting. Indeed, we transform his message in the ongoing process of gospel proclamation.

V

Israel, the Rootstock of the Church

From a historical point of view, I have suggested that the "sibling model" is the most appropriate paradigm for understanding the relationship between early Christianity and early Judaism. Not only does this model take seriously the continuing development of Judaism, but it places early Christian theological formation in the context of a dynamic and developing relationship with Jewish tradition. Paul's theology is also part of this organic process of development, a process that in his case is driven by the mission to the Gentiles. Given this historical framework, however, Paul seeks to develop a theological understanding of the relationship between the church and Israel. In other words, Paul's emerging theology of the church and Israel is developed within the context of a larger historical pattern, which I have chosen to characterize as the "sibling model" of Christian origins.

In Romans 11:16–18, toward the end of a long and tortuous discussion concerning the place of Israel in the redemptive purposes of God, Paul writes:

> If the part of the dough offered as first fruits is holy, then the whole batch is holy; and if the root is holy, then the branches also are holy. But if some of the branches were broken off, and you, a wild olive shoot, were grafted in their place to share the rich root of the olive tree, do not boast over the branches. If you do boast, remember that it is not you that support the root, but the root that supports you.

89

These remarks are aimed directly at the Gentiles among Paul's readers, and they are predicated on the assertion that God has not abandoned the people whom God foreknew. In many ways this is a stinging theological reminder to the Gentiles that they have not superseded the Jews as the people of God. The church, the Gentile church in particular, is not an independent theological entity. It has been grafted into Israel and is sustained by the richness of that theological root. This is a powerful theological image that the contemporary church, overwhelmingly Gentile in composition and influenced by generations of anti-Jewish ideology, ought to have impressed upon its conscience. Moreover, this image serves as a reminder to the church that when it disregards the theological significance of Israel, it severs itself from an important source of theological nourishment. When this occurs, the church threatens to undermine its own sense of identity and becomes ultimately an entity without a historical root.

In Romans 9–11, Paul engages in a sustained discussion of the place of Israel in the scheme of salvation and of the refusal of most Jews to believe in Christ and the gospel. These are issues that Paul cannot ignore. But they are also issues that do not lend themselves to simple solutions for Paul. Hence, these three chapters in Romans are filled with complex conceptual shifts and literary turns.[1] The reader is not always sure where the argument is headed or how the apostle intends to extricate himself from the conceptual maze that lies before him. At the end of the discourse, Paul launches into a doxology in which he acknowledges the inscrutability of God's judgments and the unsearchable character of divine ways. "For who has known the mind of the Lord? Or who has been his counselor?" (Rom. 11:34). This is Paul's way of bringing his discussion to a close. It is also his way of reminding his readers that the final word on the subject has not been written. It is to this discussion in Romans 9–11 that we now turn.

God's Word Has Not Failed

Following an anguished statement of concern for his kinfolk according to the flesh, Paul reminds his readers that to the Israelites belong the adoption as children of God, the glory, the covenants, the giving of the law, the worship, and the promises. To them belong the "patriarchs" and from them Christ according to the flesh has been born (9:1–5). Paul would even be separated from Christ if that would benefit his people. Implicit in these statements is the abiding importance of Israel for Paul and the anguish that he feels because most Jews have not believed in Christ and the gospel. But even beyond Paul's personal sense of anguish, an important theological issue is raised by the gospel's lack of success among the Jews. Has God's word itself failed?

To forestall the suggestion that the word of God has failed, Paul declares that not all Israel is Israel. To substantiate this claim, he reminds his readers of the story of Abraham and Sarah.

> And not all of Abraham's children are his true descendants; but "It is through Isaac that descendants shall be named for you." This means that it is not the children of the flesh who are the children of God, but the children of the promise are counted as descendants. (9:7–8)

This is carried through to the next generation as well. Rebecca's twin children, Jacob and Esau, are separated before they have done anything either good or bad, in order that God's purpose of election might remain. Quoting from Malachi (1:2–3), Paul concludes this segment of his discussion with the words: "I have loved Jacob, but I have hated Esau" (Rom. 9:13).

The effect of this argument has been to separate Israel from Israel, children from descendants. Paul has attempted to drive a wedge between Abraham's children and his descendants, in order to show that the people of promise are the people of election. By implication, of course, Paul has hoped to show that the word of God has not failed. God's word is not without power. But at the heart of Paul's argument is a redefinition of the historic people of Israel. "For not all Israelites truly belong to Israel" (Rom. 9:6). Circumscribed from within the people of Israel is the Israel of election. The impulse that drives this discussion is sectarianism. Paul asserts that some Jews are within Israel

and some Jews are not.[2] The children of promise are the people of
Israel according to God's election.

The fundamental issue that the apostle is compelled to discuss in
chapter 9 has to do with the Jews and their place in the purposes of
God. According to Paul's proclamation, the Messiah has come, and
faith, not Torah, is now the basis for salvation. But the vast majority of
Jews have not come to share the apostle's belief. Does this mean that
God's word has failed? As we have seen, Paul cannot accept this, for it
would portray God as ineffectual. Does it mean that God's covenant
with the Jews has been broken? Once again, Paul cannot accept this,
for it would portray God as capricious and unreliable. The issues
before Paul in Romans 9–11 certainly involve the matter of righteousness by faith, but they are precipitated by the larger concern for the
Jews and their place in God's redemptive purposes.

The distinction that Paul seeks to make in Romans 9:6–13, between
those descended from Israel and real Israel, is rooted in the notion that
there is a difference between Israel defined as a physical entity and
Israel defined as a theological concept.[3] Israel as a theological concept
is not identical, according to Paul in this argument, with Israel as a
body of people who claim common ancestry. To understand some of
the implications of this distinction, it will be helpful to compare
sectarian imagery found elsewhere in Jewish tradition.

In the Damascus Rule, found among the Dead Sea Scrolls, the
writer states: "But with the remnant which held fast to the commandments of God, He made His Covenant with Israel for ever, revealing to
them the hidden things in which all Israel had gone astray" (3:13–14).[4]
According to the writer, God has made a covenant with those among
Israel who have heeded the commandments. Implicit in this statement
is a distinction between those who are "obedient" and "all Israel." The
"obedient" make up the religious community of the writer; for him,
they as a group are distinguishable from the nation of Israel as a whole.
It is this special covenant community that is set apart theologically and
religiously from Israel as a national and physical entity. In the theology
and religious practice of this sectarian community, there is reflected an
impulse to circumscribe from within the people of Israel the "true" and
"obedient" people of God.

In a peculiar way Paul, too, reflects this impulse. His claim that there is a distinction between those descended from Israel and Israel is based on the assumption that Israel defined according to lineage is not synonymous with Israel as the people of God. Paul's use of the term Israel may not be consistent throughout Romans 9–11, but in 9:6 and in the ensuing scriptural argument it is evident that Paul seeks to emphasize the theological value of this term by focusing on the distinction between physical Israel and the promises of God. Although Paul in 9–11 retains the term Israel to describe the "unbelieving" Jews and affirms his conviction that God has not forsaken the people whom God foreknew, it is evident that for him the term "Israel" can have a special sense. Those who believe in Christ are Israel in the restricted sense of the term.

Although Paul shares with the Qumran community a similar sectarian impulse, it is clear that his claim that God has called not only Jews but Gentiles requires a distinction to be made between him and the Dead Sea covenanters. Moreover, the foundation of Qumran religious life is Torah obedience, whereas for Paul that is certainly not the case. The claim that the theological dividing line between Jews and Gentiles has been broken down and that observance of the Mosaic law is not mandatory for the inclusion of Gentiles into the community of Christ places Paul in a special category as far as Jewish religious experience is concerned.

This sectarian impulse is also played out in Paul's remnant theology in Romans 9–11. In 9:25–28, the combined citation from Hosea 2:23, 1:10, and Isaiah 10:22–23 illustrates that historical Israel has been separated into two groups. In light of 9:24, it is evident that, for Paul, the Jews whom God has called constitute the remnant that will be saved. In this discussion, the historical nation of Israel is not identical with those who have been called. Those Jews who constitute the remnant are the elect. Israel, according to Paul, has been separated into those who are included in the remnant and those who are not. Thus, the application of Isaiah 10:22–23 in the context of Romans 9:22–29 is framed by Paul's claim that Israel has been separated into two groups and that election is not limited only to Jews.

While the message of Isaiah 10:22–23 is essentially judgment, the message of Isaiah 1:9 in Romans 9:29 is reassurance in the midst of judgment and destruction. The people of God have not been betrayed as were Sodom and Gomorrah. Israel's line of descendants continues. In this passage, Paul sees his own situation. Israel is under judgment, but she has not been abandoned or destroyed. In the church, the remnant prepared for glory continues Abraham's line of descendants. This message of reassurance is emphasized once again by Paul in Romans 11:1–5. On the basis of remnant imagery from scripture, Paul has sought to announce both judgment and reassurance.

Once again, the scriptural writers are not alone in the use of remnant language to announce the preservation of God's people from complete destruction and to bring a message of hope. These themes are found in apocryphal and Qumran literature as well.[5] For example, Ben Sirach writes:

> He will never blot out the descendants of his chosen one,
>> or destroy the family line of him who loved him.
> So he gave a remnant to Jacob
>> and to David a root from his own family.
>
> (47:22)[6]

But it is perhaps with the use of this imagery at Qumran that Paul's remnant language ought to be compared. In the Qumran psalms (6:6–8) the writer states:

> And I know there is hope
>> for those who turn from transgression
>> and for those who abandon sin. . . . I am consoled for the roaring
>>> of the peoples,
>> and for the tumult of k[ing]doms when they assemble;
> [for] in a little while, I know,
>> Thou wilt raise up survivors among Thy people
>> and a remnant within Thine inheritance.[7]

In the War Rule 14:8–9, the Qumran writer states:

> But we, the remnant [of Thy people,
>> shall praise] Thy name, O God of mercies,

who hast kept the Covenant with our fathers.
In all our generations Thou hast bestowed
    Thy wonderful favours on the remnant [of Thy people]
    under the dominion of Satan.[8]

Against the background of this sectarian religious perspective, the Qumran writers use remnant language, and implicit in their use of this imagery is the differentiation between those who are part of their religious community and those who are not. The remnant will be comprised of those who are included in a particular religious group and who hold certain religious convictions. For these sectarian writers, inclusion in the remnant depends on being within a specific religious circle; the remnant within Israel will survive because it is made up of God's elect. Not only will a remnant be preserved, but this remnant is identified presently with a particular portion of Israel.

Paul, too, identifies the remnant with a specific community. For him, as for the two Qumran writers cited above, the remnant serves to differentiate groups within historical Israel. In this regard, the fundamental difference between Paul and the two Qumran writers is that the religious communities that are thought to constitute the remnant are different. Paul argues that the Jewish Christian community is evidence that God has not rejected the people whom God foreknew. In the present, a remnant has been elected by God according to grace (Rom. 11:1–5).

Paul's claim that not all Israel is Israel is framed in terms of Jewish biblical and religious tradition. By setting apart from within the nation of Israel the people of God, Paul has drawn on broader Jewish impulses. He has used these impulses to redefine the people of God, and he has sought to show that God has not rejected God's people. This is the apostle's way of seeking to reconcile the historic promises to Israel and the soteriological claims of the church. Paul, the Jew and apostle of Christ, is committed to both. But as a practical religious matter, Paul is compelled to address the issue of God's power and faithfulness. In so doing, he turns to the scriptures to an extent that is unprecedented in his letters. Furthermore, as we have seen, Paul attempts to use the Abraham/Sarah material to differentiate the descendants of the patriarch from his children (heirs). The apostle certainly did not draw conclusions that would have met with approval among the vast majority of Jewish people. Still, he made use of concepts and impulses that were thoroughly embedded in Jewish scripture and experience.

Despite a detour in 9:14–23 to deal with the issue of God's justice, an issue precipitated by the argument in 9:6–13, Paul's overriding concern in this section of the discourse is the efficacy of God's word. The discussion in 9:1–29 is not an argument against Israel, and it is not an argument against the Jews, although Paul is clearly troubled by their lack of faith in Christ. It is rather Paul's attempt to pick his way through the thorny problems of God's faithfulness to Israel, the identification of the people of promise, and the efficacy of the divine word.

For the Christian community, these issues are still important. And they ought to be considered anew in each theological generation of the church. Paul, for his part, is adamant that God has not abandoned the Jews. They have not been rejected. Moreover, God's word has not failed, and God's promises continue. These are important pillars upon which the church must base its ongoing theological reflection. When these have been forgotten, the history of the church has often taken an anti-Jewish turn. Not only has that had horrific consequences for the Jews, but it has had morally negative consequences for the church as well. Furthermore, when Christianity came to be an independent religion and Paul came to be read from the perspective of an outsider to Judaism, he has often become an ally in the disparagement of Judaism and the Jewish people. That is why it is imperative that Paul be understood in the context of Judaism. When he is unwittingly extracted from that context, he can no longer challenge the anti-Semitic inclinations of the modern world and of much historic Christian theology. In that event, Paul ceases to be an engaging conversation partner and in fact may be made an accomplice in the church's tendency toward anti-Judaism.

Righteousness, Works of Law, and Faith

In Romans 9:30, Paul's discussion shifts direction. He writes: "What then are we to say? Gentiles, who did not strive for righteousness, have attained it, that is, righteousness through faith; but Israel, who did strive for the righteousness that is based on the law, did not succeed in fulfilling that law. Why not? Because they did not strive for it on the basis of faith, but as if it were based on works" (9:30–32). Israel has not pursued righteousness according to faith but according to works. That, according to Paul, is its mistake. The focus of the discussion in 9:30–32 is not primarily Israel's refusal to believe in Christ but its failure to distinguish two types of righteousness. It is not so much a matter of the law being wrong or bad as it is a matter of Israel pursuing the law in the wrong way.[9] This argument is, of course, predicated on the discussion of righteousness by faith found elsewhere in Romans and Galatians.

In 10:1–4, Paul once again shows his feelings for the people of Israel. His wish and prayer is that they may obtain salvation. While Paul concedes that the Jews have zeal for God, it is not according to "knowledge." Presumably, Paul means that they have shown zeal for the law but unfortunately have sought to attain righteousness by works and not by faith. They sought to establish their own righteousness, instead of submitting to the righteousness of God. Once again, the larger Pauline context for this discussion is Paul's conviction that the Gentiles ought to be included in the community of Christ by faith and not obedience to the law. In other words they need not become Jews first. The law is not an entrance requirement into the community of Christ.

Verses 5–8, important in their own right,[10] also serve as a transition from the discussion of righteousness to a discussion of proclamation, faith, confession, and salvation. This leads to the statement in 10:12–13: "For there is no distinction between Jew and Greek; the same Lord is Lord of all and is generous to all who call upon him. For, 'Everyone who calls on the name of the Lord shall be saved.' " The repeated use of "all" in these verses emphasizes the universal character of the Pauline gospel. It also sets the stage for the claim that the word of Christ has gone out into all the world but not all have heeded its message. The word has gone forth, says Paul. Preachers have been sent to proclaim the "good news," but the fact remains that not all have believed the proclamation of the Christian evangelists. The "unbelief" of Israel cannot be attributed to having never heard the word of faith and the proclamation of Christ. Israel's "unbelief" is not due to the failure of God's word (9:6). Chapter 10 concludes with a series of scriptural quotations (Ps. 19:4, Deut. 32:21, and Isa. 65:1–2) that emphasize the universality of the proclamation of Christ, the inclusion of Gentiles, the jealousy of Israel, and finally the contrariness of Israel in the face of God's beckoning. From a discussion of righteousness early in chapter 10 to a scriptural declaration of Israel's disobedience at the close of the chapter, Paul has clearly struggled with the "unbelief" of the Jews. If the argument were to end on this note, one would probably have to conclude that, for Paul, Israel has fallen under the condemnation and wrath of God. Perhaps God has abandoned Israel and the Jews. Perhaps they have been rejected once and for all.

Paul, of course, does not end his discussion at this point. His commitment to righteousness by faith and to belief in Christ is beyond question. Furthermore, he is truly troubled by Israel's lack of faith in Christ and by its brand of adherence to the law. But for theological reasons—and I would argue religious reasons as well—the apostle is not inclined to sever the church from Israel. Had he done so, many of his theological problems would have been removed. The very fact that Paul steadfastly refused to do this, as seen in chapter 11, argues for the necessity of the discussion in Romans 10. It reminds the reader of Romans that Christology identifies Paul as a special variety of Jew. It also reminds us of the difficult position of having to maintain the abiding character of God's covenant with the Jews and at the same time of highlighting God's work of salvation in Jesus Christ for all, Jew and Gentile alike. The personal anguish that this causes Paul and the theological dilemma that this sets before him are perhaps nowhere more evident than in Romans 10. Attempts to minimize this difficulty do disservice to Paul and his epistles.

This portion of Paul's argument stands as a historic reminder to religious Jews and Christians that beneath everything else it is the Torah and the figure of Christ that both unite and separate them. Is the Torah central? Or is it peripheral? How does it function? Jesus was a Jew, but how does the Christ of faith figure into the religion of Judaism? Is faith in Christ necessary for the salvation of Israel? These are questions that were on Paul's theological agenda; and they are, I suggest, from the Christian point of view still important questions for the church's process of self-identification and self-understanding. This chapter in Paul's epistle to the Romans continues to call the church back to these hard theological questions, both as a prod and as a gauge of how and where the church is moving theologically. Far from bringing Christianity's conversation with Judaism to an end, Paul in a rather curious way forces us to keep the questions open and the conversation alive.

And So All Israel Will Be Saved

Paul makes two things clear at the beginning of chapter 11: God has not rejected the chosen people, and God has not foreclosed the prospect of their salvation. They have not stumbled so as to fall, says Paul (11:11). Instead, he seeks to give positive value and purpose to the "unbelief" of Israel. "But through their stumbling salvation has come to the Gentiles so as to make Israel jealous" (11:11). Using the idea of jealousy, first introduced into the discussion in 10:19, Paul sketches his vision of salvation-history. The gospel, having met resistance among the Jews, has gone forth to the Gentiles with the hope that Israel will finally see what it has missed. Paul views his own apostolic mission to the Gentiles as part of this process. The trespass of Israel has been important for the world and for the Gentiles, but even more significant will be Israel's inclusion or "fullness." This, then, is the context for the Pauline analogies in 11:13–24.

Realizing the negative effect his words may have, especially on the Gentiles, Paul in turn directs his remarks specifically to them. As if to remind his Gentile readers, he declares that if the dough offered as first fruits is holy so is the whole lump, and if the root is holy so are the branches. Various suggestions have been made as to the referent of the terms "first fruits" and "root"—patriarchs, Abraham, Adam[11]—with the terms "lump" and "branches" in 11:16 referring then to Israel. Regardless of the specific referents one may wish to assign, these analogies clearly serve to enhance the theological role, and perhaps even the primacy, of Israel in the scope of salvation-history. The Jews, even the "unbelieving" Jews, as part of Israel, are holy.

Paul's argument is carried still further in 11:17–24. Switching metaphors, Paul distinguishes two types of branches, the wild and the tame. He clearly wants to remind the Gentiles that they are the wild branches that have been grafted into the olive tree. They are the outsiders who have been included, contrary to all natural expectations. They have no reason to be high-minded about their place in the history of salvation. They have no reason to boast about their inclusion in the community of God's people. The Gentiles who have been included do not support the root, rather they are supported *by* the root. Paul writes in 11:24 in conclusion to his discussion: "For if you have been cut from what is by nature a wild olive tree and grafted, contrary to nature, into a cultivated olive tree, how much more will these natural branches be grafted back into their own olive tree." The function of this metaphor is surely to remind the Gentiles of the derivative nature of their place in salvation-history and to forestall the possibility that Gentiles will exalt themselves at the expense of their Jewish brothers and sisters. Paul, of course, is not inclined to disregard the "unbelief" of the Jews, but he clearly seeks to put it into a larger perspective. In doing this, he emphasizes the "natural" priority of Israel and the "unnatural" status of the Gentiles in God's work of salvation.

In 11:25–26, Paul informs his readers of what he chooses to call a mystery. As the New Revised Standard Version translates the Greek text, this is done "so that you may not claim to be wiser than you are." Paul declares that a hardness has come upon part of Israel until the full number of the Gentiles come in and thus all Israel will be saved. These verses raise several exegetical issues. Does Paul mean that every individual Jew will be saved? Or does he understand the term "Israel" in a corporate, theological sense? Will all the Jews finally be brought to faith in Christ? Or does Israel have a special track to salvation, perhaps even apart from Christ? These questions have all been raised and debated with respect to the interpretation of 11:25–26. Given the arguments in chapter 10 and earlier in chapter 11, it seems rather improbable to me that Paul intends to imply that Israel has a special track to salvation apart from Christ. Moreover, the expression "all Israel" does not necessarily mean that every individual Jew will be saved through conversion to Christ.[12] It may be that Paul intends to suggest that the "fullness" of Israel will be saved when the full number of the Gentiles has been included.

Regardless of the specific exegetical answers that one gives to these questions, however, Paul makes clear that Israel is fundamentally important to his theology and that God has not abandoned the Jews. He is especially concerned that the Gentile followers of Christ not be overcome by their own conceit and pride. Gentile Christianity is not, according to Paul, an independent phenomenon. It has been grafted into the rootstock of Israel and in that way shares the richness of the tree. Gentiles ought not to be deceived into thinking that they have theological pride of place in the history of salvation. Furthermore, this entire discussion is really an internal Christian debate. For Jews, the issues that have been under consideration throughout most of chapters 9–11 would not have been issues of concern. These issues would simply not have arisen for most Jewish people.

Conclusion

Contemporary interpreters of Paul's argument in Romans 9–11 might be inclined to approach the text with a one-dimensional exegetical question: What does the Pauline text mean? Or, to cast the question a bit more widely, what does Paul say about the salvation of the Jews? Armed with this question, the interpreter seeks to answer exegetically the question that has been posed. On one level, this is perhaps the way the interpretive enterprise ought to be undertaken. The text of Romans is critically analyzed, and the meaning of the argument is simply extracted from the text. Once this has been accomplished, the determined meaning of the text can be either accepted or rejected as theologically relevant. If it is accepted as relevant, it may also be used as one of the pillars upon which to build a Christian theology of Judaism.

However, the conversation model of interpretation and, I would argue, the character of Romans 9–11 itself suggest a more complex way of engaging these three chapters. To be sure, the text ought to be studied critically and with rigor but not simply from the point of view of extracting *the* meaning of the text. The interpretive encounter with the text results in the construction of a framework of meaning. As we have seen, Paul was confronted with a theological problem, and he turned to his sacred texts in order to address that problem. The result of this process was not merely the citation of certain biblical references and the simple discernment of their meaning. On the contrary, the biblical quotations came to be used and interpreted by Paul as part of his effort to develop a persuasive and theologically satisfying response to the issue of Israel's "unbelief." The way Paul employed his biblical citations and the way he wove them into his discussion involved the merging of the scriptural texts with his own apostolic context and theological concern. They have come together in a mutually informing encounter.

The interpretive "ground rules" for Paul's encounter with scripture are not the same as the "ground rules" for our conversations with scripture, but his discussion does suggest something significant to us about the dynamics of interpretation. We are invited into an interpretive conversation, from the point of view of our own context, with the text, in this case Romans 9–11. Moreover, from a Christian theological perspective, the task is not simply to repeat what we think Paul is saying in these three chapters but to use them as one component, perhaps even a springboard, in our own evolving reflections on Christianity's relationship with Judaism. This approach keeps the interpretive conversation going on many different levels. A premium is placed on the open-ended character of the conversation. Anything that effectively ends this conversation is fatal to interpretation, indeed perhaps to theology itself. In Romans 9–11, Paul did not pronounce the final word on the subject of Israel, Christ, and the word of God. Rather, he contributed to the church's ongoing conversation on the subject and implicitly invited those who were to come after him to enter into this conversation as well. This invitation is displayed in the dialogic character of Paul's discussion and in the concluding doxology. The discourse in 9–11 is not so much a treatise as it is an attempt, given certain parameters, to devise a way of understanding the issue at hand.

As troubled as Paul is by the "unbelief" of Israel, he holds steadfastly to the conviction that, in one form or another, God's covenant with Israel remains in force. Israel has not been abandoned, and it has not been replaced by a new Israel. This is arguably the most conspicuous feature of Paul's discussion, certainly in chapters 9 and 11. Indeed, it might well be the case that this is the most appropriate starting point for present-day theological reflection on Christianity's relation to the religion of Judaism. Gentile Christianity has been grafted into Israel, and theologically it is this metaphor that identifies the proper place of Christianity with respect to Judaism. To state the issue even more clearly, New Testament Christianity makes little or no theological sense apart from Israel and Judaism. Jesus, the central figure in the Christian drama, was a Jew and not a Christian. And the New Testament documents are heavily reliant on Jewish texts (the Hebrew scriptures) and concepts. Thus, both in terms of historical reality and theological abstraction, it is appropriate to see the early Jesus movement as an outgrowth of early Judaism. Furthermore, Paul presents us with an appropriate image for understanding Gentile Christianity's theological relationship to Israel. Christianity has been incorporated into Israel. The church today, largely Gentile, would do well to heed the warning about high-mindedness and conceit in its thinking about and dealings with Judaism. This warning is made even more acute in light of centuries of Christian anti-Judaism. To disregard the church's theological relationship with Israel is tantamount to disregarding the very rootstock from which the church itself springs.

Historic Judaism in its various forms, however, makes good sense apart from Christianity. But since the fourth-century political success of the church in the West, Judaism has not often had the privilege of ignoring Christianity and Christians.[13] Because of its minority status, Judaism has been forced to take Christianity seriously. Not necessarily for theological reasons but for social, political, and economic reasons, Judaism has had to confront Christianity and its cultural influence. Christians, on the other hand, could treat Jews as a mere nuisance when it suited their purposes and could vilify them when they sought a scapegoat. Had Christians taken more seriously their own theological rootstock, such attitudes toward Judaism and Jews might not have been allowed to prevail. Paul's discussion in Romans 9–11 stands as a warning to the church against taking such a callous and theologically suspect approach to Judaism and to Jews. Perhaps the surest way for Christians to heed this warning is to maintain an ongoing conversation with Judaism and with Jews, a conversation marked by respect and honesty as well as by serious investigation of the respective traditions.

VI
Adam and Christ:
Point and Counterpoint

Theologians frequently engage in dialectical forms of comparison. Christ stands opposite Adam, the church stands opposite the world, the believer stands opposite the unbeliever—and I have argued here that in hermeneutical theory the text and the interpreter form the dialectic of the interpretive conversation. There is nothing unique to the Bible or religion about this form of reasoning. It is simply a way of understanding an object, event, or concept in relation to its opposite or apparent opposite. Just as human beings use analogical forms of thinking to understand an object, event, or concept, so we also use reverse forms of analogy. Figure A is like figure B in this regard and unlike figure B in that regard. While historical considerations may indeed come into play in dialectical forms of reasoning, it is not primarily history, generally conceived, that governs this manner of thinking. Structural similarities and dissimilarities between figures enable this form of reasoning to make sense and become operative in the human mind. In dialectical forms of reasoning, the "one" is always defined in relation to the "other." It is this relational quality that must be identified if the dialectic is to be helpful and illustrative.

Paul uses Adam and Christ as dialectical figures. They are opposite and yet they are not opposite. There is something similar about them, just as there is something in reality dissimilar about them. The similarity and the dissimilarity between Adam and Christ are discovered in the relational interplay between the two figures. Paul herme-

105

neutically engages the two images and in so doing constructs a dialectic in which an aspect of his conception of reality is illustrated. While the temporal distinctions between Adam and Christ never recede completely from Paul's view, they are secondary to the structural relationships between them. Adam and Christ, according to Paul, represent two forms of humanity.

The Christian community cannot be understood simply in terms of its essence, represented historically and ontologically. It is identified dialectically, indeed relationally. The church is defined and identified in terms of the "other"; it is understood in relation to its synonym and its antonym. In this way, we discover what the church is and is not in relation to something else (for example, culture). We discover who Christ is and is not in relation to his opposite (Adam). We come to understand life in relation to death, sin in relation to grace, transgression in relation to gift, and so on. Multiple opposites are juxtaposed as a means of understanding something about the structure of redemptive reality. One perhaps might also claim that an individual's faith or commitment to God, too, must in the end be understood in relation to its opposite. Life in Christ (the sphere of Christ humanity) is understood in relation to life in Adam (the sphere of Adamic humanity). To take this a step further, the figures in the dialectic do not make sense apart from their opposite. What is life apart from death? What is grace apart from sin? What is belief apart from unbelief? What is Christ apart from Adam? As concepts and realities, these make sense primarily in relation to their opposites. Remove its opposite and the figure becomes more or less unintelligible. In other words, Christ, as well as life in the sphere of humanity represented by Christ, must not be divorced from its opposite reality. To do so is to render Christ and that which Christ represents less intelligible conceptually and probably superfluous theologically. Does Christ have significance apart from Adam?

Paul's use of the two figures, Adam and Christ, often gets bogged down theologically in questions of original sin. Augustine certainly made use of these texts in the formulation of his notions of sin,[1] but here I propose to view these Pauline texts in terms of their dialectical relationships. Romans 5:12–21, far from highlighting an Augustinian concept of original sin, focuses our attention on the dialectical relationship between two forms of humanity, those represented by Christ and Adam. In 1 Corinthians 15:45–49, the dialectic turns on the relationship between the first Adam and the last Adam. In both texts, the christological development proceeds according to patterns of opposition predicated on certain underlying connections between the two figures. It is this relational form of christological thinking that drives Paul. Hence, he uses these two figures and the concepts associated with them to illustrate something about the very nature of human existence, defined both in terms of Adam and Christ.

Adam, a Type of the One to Come

In Romans 5:12–21, Adam is portrayed as a type of the one to come. The word *typos* is used by Paul to indicate the relationship between Adam and Christ. In this context, the word *typos* is perhaps best understood as "model" or "pattern."[2] Adam and Christ are not identical but are held in a typological relationship that has its unity in the understanding that Adam stands at the head of humanity lost in sin and death and Christ stands at the head of humanity born anew in righteousness. The foundation of Paul's typology rests on the conviction that there are two basic spheres of humanity.

Adam, the historical figure associated with the Fall, sin, and ultimately death, represents humanity under the sway of death. For Paul, this power is clearly a contemporary reality. It is not limited to the ancient past, and it is not limited to the mythic figure of Adam. In Romans 5:12, the apostle presents his view of the sin that came into the world through Adam and the sins that all people commit. The former appears to be a deed insofar as Adam transgressed the commandment of God. But Adam's sin is more than a single act. It is a power that has determinative control over humankind. Through the act of disobedience, Adam is portrayed as turning human history over to the rule of death. In this regard, Adam is not to be considered simply as a representative of humanity. He is the one who stands at the head of fallen humanity and who is thought to share fully in it. Paul points to Adam as the origin of sin and death (see Gen. 3:1–7, 19). But sin is not, according to Paul, something that can be attributed solely to the misfortune of Adam's act of disobedience.

Humanity participates in the rule of sin and death and in a sense continues to establish the rule of Adam by its own transgression. The apostle sets forth the relationship between the sin in which humanity shares because of Adam's transgression and the sin that all people share because of their own transgressions. Humankind has been consigned to the realm of sin and death and also consigns itself to the realm of sin and death. In Paul's argument, there is a tension between the inevitability of sin and the responsibility for it.

Although Paul's argument is driven dialectically, he becomes entangled in an attempt to explain the nature of Adam's sin and the sin of pre-Mosaic humanity as distinguished from the sin of humanity under the law. Paul's dilemma is that he asserts the priority and universality of the sin of Adam, yet he has a concept of law that accords to it the increase of sin. The problem arises because Paul uses temporal categories to explain a power that he believes exists also as a present dialectical reality. The rule of Adam is not simply a phenomenon locked in the past. The effects of Adam's transgression persist into the present. Paul, however, understands that the law poses a formal difficulty for his discussion. While pre-Mosaic humanity did not live under the law of Moses, it still lived under the influence of Adam's transgression. Therefore, the question could reasonably be addressed to Paul: What is the difference between the sin of pre-Mosaic humankind and the sin of humankind under the law? On the one hand, the apostle asserts that sin and death were in the world from Adam to Moses because the rule of sin had come into the world through Adam. With his understanding of the law, however, Paul cannot stop at this point. He is compelled by the demands of consistency to assert that sin and transgression prior to Moses are somehow different from sin and transgression after Moses. He concludes that apart from the law sin is not charged or counted. If sin and death ruled before Moses as well as after Moses, the only difference according to Paul is that under the law sin is "charged to one's account."

In 5:14, Paul states: "Yet death exercised dominion from Adam to

Moses, even over those whose sins were not like the transgression of Adam, who is a type of the one who was to come." J. A. T. Robinson has written that the one who is to come is not Christ but Moses or simply humankind under the law.[3] If this interpretation were to be accepted, the entire dialectical relationship between Adam and Christ as developed in 5:12–21 would make little sense. The underlying connection that Paul is seeking to establish is between Adam and Christ and not between Adam and Moses. Only against the background of the Adam/Christ dialectical relationship and the spheres of humanity indicated by them is Moses introduced into the discussion. Moses is mentioned simply as a representative of the law that presents a formal difficulty for the apostle's view of sin and death. Hence, there seems little doubt that Paul intends to present Adam as a negative precursor of Christ.

Having established the underlying connection between Adam and Christ, the apostle is compelled to contrast the two primary figures of his discussion. Paul begins the contrast by asserting that the free gift is not like the trespass. In other words, the gift of grace brought into the world by Christ is not like the transgression of Adam. The reader is led to expect that Adam and Christ will be contrasted simply in terms of a negative correspondence. But Paul does not proceed in this way. In the course of the argument, Paul redirects the discussion away from an analogy to an argument that proceeds from a "minor to a major cause."[4] The expression *pollō mallon* ("how much more"), which Paul uses on numerous occasions in his letters, serves to contrast the gift of grace in Christ and the transgression of Adam on the basis of degree. That which is true in the case of Adam (minor cause) is far surpassed in the case of Christ (major cause). Many have died through Adam's trespass, but the grace of God abounds much more for the "many" through Jesus Christ. The presupposition in this contrast for Paul is that Adam and Christ have a typological, indeed dialectical, relationship as both stand at the head of their respective lines of humanity. In this regard, the two figures are not different in kind.[5] However, the "free gift" and the "transgression" are contrasted in degree in such a manner that they are shown to be qualitatively different.

The "how much more" form of contrast is a typically Jewish (though not only Jewish) method of presenting an argument.[6] In this regard, it is a technical form of argumentation, and for that reason it should not be assumed that Paul is operating only on the level of the theoretical or theological. In one sense, Paul is simply conforming to a Jewish interpretive convention. Yet interpretive conventions are intended to generate and convey ideas that have meaning. Thus, the "how much more" method of argumentation is placed in the service of an attempt to contrast Adam and Christ. Christ and the free gift are not finally the same as Adam and the transgression. To the extent that grace surpasses the trespass of Adam in power and effect, it is also qualitatively different. Paul does not intend to represent Adam and Christ as the two poles of a cosmic dualism. The gift of grace is different in that which it effects and is categorically different in its power.[7] The power of Christ's gift surpasses beyond measure the power of Adam's transgression. Instead of arguing that Christ is simply Adam's antonym, Paul distinguishes Christ and what Christ represents by the extent to which they surpass Adam and what he represents. Thus, Adam and Christ are structurally linked, but at the same time they are fundamentally different.

In Romans 5:15, Paul makes clear that through the trespass of the one man, Adam, "many" have died. While in this verse the apostle does not state what results for the "many" from the gift of grace, it is clearly implied that life is the result. Into the power of death that rules through Adam, Christ has come and established the rule of life. As if to emphasize and establish this point, Paul writes in verse 17: "If, because of the one man's trespass, death exercised dominion through that one, much more surely will those who receive the abundance of grace and the free gift of righteousness exercise dominion in life through the one man, Jesus Christ." While Adam is the man of death, Christ is the man of life. Not only is that which they do contrasted, but so is that which is effected for humanity by their actions. Adam's transgression brings about death but also judgment and condemnation. Likewise, the free gift of grace in Christ brings righteousness as well as life. That which has been effected through Christ is opposite and categorically different from that which rules in the sphere of Adam. Between Adam and Christ there is an inherent opposition. But even more, Christ brings about a reversal of the Fall and disobedience of Adam.[8] "The free gift following many trespasses brings justification," writes Paul in 5:16. Into a world lost in sin and under condemnation, Christ has come and has established the rule of life and righteousness. With Adam as the dialectical foil, Paul has highlighted what he perceives to be the significance of Christ and his work.

This rather lengthy discussion has served to illustrate our argument from another perspective. Paul has sought to amplify his vision of Christ by using Adam as an agent of comparison and contrast. It seems quite probable that Adam is not the primary object of Paul's concern, but as a scriptural figure he gives the apostle a point of reference for comprehending a christological form of human existence, which stands opposite life conformed to the figure of Adam. Two things occur in the dynamic of Paul's argument. First, the apostle sees Adam in light of his christologically formed view of the world. Through his transgression of the commandment of God, Adam has affected the future course of human affairs. Redemption, by contrast, involves a reversal of that which has come to pass through Adam. For Paul, Christ becomes the agent of that reversal. Christ becomes the one who highlights the human predicament that has resulted from the disobedience of Adam, and at the same time Christ counters the power of sin and death. Second, Christ as savior makes little sense unless there is someone who has done what Adam did or unless the state of human affairs is in need of being transformed. Thus, it may be almost impossible for Paul to conceive of Christology at all apart from an Adamic fall and a cosmic power of sin and death. Not only would Christ be superfluous apart from Adam, but he would be virtually incomprehensible as a spiritual redeemer and savior. Hence, Paul does not merely see Adam in light of his convictions about Christ, but Adam gives a context of meaning for understanding Christ as redeemer. Apart from that context, Christ may be, at best, meaningless and, at worst, irrelevant.

I suggest that Paul's use of the biblical imagery in Romans 5:12–21 is not characterized simply by an attempt to uncover the true significance of the material. Rather, it is an attempt to use the scriptural symbolism as a way of generating a dialectical argument.

The apostle manipulates the biblical images and uses them to establish a set of christological images. These christological images then expand the conceptual horizon of the apostle and those to whom he is writing. Paul seeks to form a christological worldview that involves a dialectical understanding of human existence. Hence, Romans 5:12–21 is not so much an attempt to search the scriptural material for truth as it is to use the Genesis imagery as a means of creating a framework of truth. In this process, the Adamic imagery of Genesis encounters the messianic conviction of the apostle and a set of christological images emerges, which becomes part of the church's conceptual framework and religious tradition. Christ is understood in relation to his counterpart, and life in Christ is understood in relation to its opposite. By seeing them dialectically, Adam and Christ (and also what they represent) serve to define each other. They are understood relative to one another.

First Adam and Last

From a chronological point of view, the discussion in Romans 5:12–21 is preceded by the apostle's excursus on the resurrection in 1 Corinthians 15. The argument in 1 Corinthians foreshadows the more complete treatment of the relationship between Adam and Christ in Romans 5. Unlike the later discussion in Romans, Paul in 1 Corinthians identifies the first man as Adam, whereas Christ is described as the second man or the last Adam. He writes:

> "The first man, Adam, became a living being"; the last Adam became a life-giving spirit. . . . The first man was from the earth, a man of dust; the second man is from heaven. As was the man of dust, so are those who are of the dust; and as is the man of heaven, so are those who are of heaven.
>
> (1 Cor. 15:45, 47–48)

There is evidence that the heavenly man/earthly man contrast was already current in first-century Judaism,[9] and it is likely that Paul was aware of this contrasting imagery when he wrote to the church in Corinth. Nevertheless, it is evident that Paul has employed a dialectical argument to differentiate Adam and Christ. While the first Adam became a living being, the last Adam became a life-giving spirit. In the language of the text, the two figures are linked by the words "life" and "living." Both are connected with life. The first Adam is viewed in terms of physical life and the second Adam in terms of a spirit that gives life. It should be noted that the focus of this discussion is not on the first Adam's act of disobedience but on his legendary position as the first living human being (contrast 1 Cor. 15:21–22). Moreover, the apostle proceeds to distinguish Adam, the man of dust from the earth, and Christ, the man from heaven. While this distinction serves to characterize the two Adams, its more important function is to establish the origins of the man of dust and the man of heaven. As the argument moves subtly to the origins of the two Adams, it also becomes clear to the reader that Paul is interested in establishing the destination of the man of dust and the man of heaven. In other words, the physical creature returns to the earth and the heavenly creature abides in immortality. "Just as we have borne the image of the man of dust, we will also bear the image of the man of heaven" (1 Cor. 15:49). Drawing on the imagery of Genesis 3:19, Paul seeks to illustrate that a person's bodily nature does not inherit the kingdom of God. But even as the physical body shares the same fate as the first Adam, so the "believer" shall also share the imperishable nature of the heavenly man, the second Adam.

Unlike Paul's argument in Romans 5:12–21, the discussion in 1 Corinthians is played out against the background of the resurrection of the dead. This means that, in the structure of the argument in 1 Corinthians, Adam is contrasted with Christ in terms of the character of life that ensues from each and in terms of the ultimate destination of human nature. The focus is not simply a delineation of two spheres of humanity. Rather, Adam functions as an image in 1 Corinthians that serves to distinguish the mortal from the immortal. The man of dust is distinguished from the man of heaven. In the conceptual framework of the discourse, Christ becomes the life-giving spirit that is at work in the transformation from mortality to immortality. This transformation is what Paul signifies by the term "resurrection," when he writes:

> So it is with the resurrection of the dead. What is sown is perishable,
> what is raised is imperishable. It is sown in dishonor, it is raised in glory.
> It is sown in weakness, it is raised in power. It is sown a physical body, it
> is raised a spiritual body.   (1 Cor. 15:42–44)

In this "argument of opposites," Paul uses Adam and Christ to illustrate the expected transformation from the perishable physical body to the imperishable spiritual body of the "believer." Once again, the contrasting figures are understood relative to each other.

According to Paul, the future expectation of the resurrection of the dead is predicated upon the conviction that Christ himself has been raised from the grave.[10] In 1 Corinthians 15:20–21, he states: "But in fact Christ has been raised from the dead, the first fruits of those who have died. For since death came through a human being, the resurrection of the dead has also come through a human being." In this text, there is no emphasis upon Adam as a living being. Instead, Adam is viewed as the agent through whom death has come into the world, just as Christ is the agent through whom resurrection has come.[11] The focus of the discussion is, of course, the resurrection of Christ and its relation to the anticipated resurrection of the "faithful." Unlike the discussion in the later verses of the chapter, there is no use of first-Adam and last-Adam language. The figures are simply viewed as opposites. One is the agent of death and the other is the agent of resurrection and life.

Conclusion

It has been suggested that Adam is not the ultimate object of Paul's concern in Romans 5:12–21 or 1 Corinthians 15:20–21, 45–49. On the contrary, Adam serves as the dialectical foil against which Paul's Christology is conceived and highlighted. Both as the progenitor of humanity lost in death and as the progenitor of the human race, Adam is juxtaposed with Christ who then becomes a life-giving spirit, the agent of redeemed humanity, and the one who stands at the head of humanity established in righteousness. Christ and what he represents are defined in terms of their opposite number. Indeed, they are structurally linked with their opposite. That is what makes the dialectic work. In no sense, however, does Christ fully assume the role and function of Adam. In terms of the conversation model of interpretation, Adam and Christ represent polar opposites. As two poles of the dialectic, Adam and Christ have something in common. But in terms of character and function the two can only be seen as representing opposite and contrasting phenomena. In this context, Paul uses the figure of Adam as a springboard to generate his discussion of who Christ is and what he has done. By highlighting Christ's opposite number, Paul presents the reader with a dialectical vantage point from which to view Christ's redemption and the resurrection of the dead.

If the Pauline christological perspectives in Romans 5 and 1 Corinthians 15 do not seem particularly provocative or novel to us today, it is probably because much of Christianity has already been thoroughly infused with images that are implicit in the apostle's arguments. But only against the backdrop of centuries of theological development can Paul's christological worldview possibly be considered banal or self-evident. To see Jesus as the last Adam or to view the Messiah as a spiritual Redeemer or to associate the Messiah with the "bodily" resurrection of the dead would not have been obvious connections to make in the first century. They required the mind of a person who was able to take the traditions of his people, shape them into a christological framework, and at the same time use those religious and biblical traditions to elaborate the early church's incipient Christology. In this regard, Paul exhibits both flexibility of mind and the tenacity of an ardent believer.

The argument in Romans 5:12–21 ultimately transcends temporal categories. It is not finally an argument about the first sin or about original sin. Moreover, the figure of Moses is not at the heart of the matter either. It is an existential argument about two forms of humanity. To interpret this text primarily in terms of original sin is to miss this dialectic. It is to ignore the existential character of the text. And it is finally to allow the sin of Adam to take precedence over the free gift made available in Christ. This is precisely what Paul does not do in this text. The free gift far surpasses the death that was brought into the world by Adam's trespass. For Paul, the community of faith and individuals within that community live in a dialectical relationship. To dissolve this dialectic would be either to emphasize, out of proportion, a "sin-oriented" theology or to hold to a view of Christ that is superfluous. In both cases, the "good news" of life and righteousness is undermined. The gospel is either depreciated or trivialized.

Paul's existential understanding of these two forms of humanity is important theologically. The gospel is to be understood in terms of its opposite. Indeed, these opposites are at work in the world and in the church. They are at work in individuals. How better to understand the wonder of life than to understand death? How better to understand righteousness than to understand unrighteousness and condemnation? How better to understand obedience than to understand transgression? How better to understand the free gift than to understand bondage to sin? Indeed, the one cannot be understood apart from the other. Life, righteousness, obedience, and the free gift, however, must finally prevail over death, unrighteousness, transgression, and bondage to sin. That is the historic hope and testimony of the Pauline church. To turn this around can in the end lead to despair and hopelessness.

Paul writes:

> For as all die in Adam, so all will be made alive in Christ. . . . So it is with the resurrection of the dead. What is sown is perishable, what is raised is imperishable. It is sown in dishonor, it is raised in glory. It is sown in weakness, it is raised in power. It is sown a physical body, it is raised a spiritual body. (1 Cor. 15:22, 42–44)

The contrasts serve to distinguish what is sown from what is raised, what dies from what is resurrected. In these paired figures, the reality of the present is contrasted with the reality of the future. Life is contrasted with death. Paul's hope for the future is anchored in life and not death; it is anchored in glory and not dishonor; it is anchored in power and not weakness.

VII

Torah, Wisdom, and Christ: Recentering the Divine Drama

In the ancient Jewish religious drama, Moses and the wandering people of Israel are portrayed as receiving the commandments from God on Mount Sinai. The covenant sealed by the law is established; the people are bound to their God by the gracious gift of Torah. God has revealed this gift to the people of God's own choosing, and they have made the law a centerpiece of their religion. The legal substance of Judaism is Torah, and the practice of Judaism is obedience to Torah. For the implications of Torah, the scriptures are studied and the traditions of the people are searched, discussed, and debated. Ultimately the Torah, both the written and the oral Torah, came to define the character and activity of Jews who live under the guidance of the rabbis.

But Torah is not simply the law of God; it is also identified among ancient Jews as the wisdom of God. It is God's wisdom made known to the people of Israel.

> I [wisdom] came forth from the mouth of the Most High,
>> and covered the earth like a mist. . . .
> Then the Creator of all things gave me a command,
>> and my Creator chose the place for my tent.
> He said, "Make your dwelling in Jacob,
>> and in Israel receive your inheritance."   (Sir. 24:3, 8)

In personal terms, the wisdom of God is described as the covenant of the Most High God, the law that Moses commanded (Sir. 24:23).

117

Wisdom/Torah is a central religious reality in the "story" of Judaism. It is the ultimate expression of God's covenant, which the sages seek and strive to obtain. It is dynamic and not static. It is thought to epitomize the relationship that God has with God's people and with the world.

On the road to Damascus, something happened to Paul that changed his life. Jesus was revealed to him as the Christ, the Son of God, says the apostle. This conviction led him finally to the conclusion that Jesus is also the wisdom of God, the gift of God to Jews and Gentiles alike. As the *telos* ("end," "goal") of the law, Christ also begins to assume the symbolism of Torah. The imagery of Torah is clearly linked with the figure of Christ (Rom. 10:6–8). He becomes the expression of God's revelation. That which has been written about Torah in scripture can now be understood, according to Paul, to pertain to Christ. For Christ's followers, he has become the focal point of humankind's relationship with God. This was a conviction that most Jews, of course, did not share. However, it was this christological claim that came to undergird the Pauline view of redemption and its ritual practice.

As Paul's religious framework shifted, so did his interpretive framework. If the primary link between heaven and earth was no longer thought to be the temple or Torah but Christ instead, the interpretation of scriptural symbolism was also bound to shift. In fact, these interpretive shifts manifested underlying religious and theological shifts. In certain examples, this process actually involved a christological recentering of the tradition. It involved a christological reapplication of scriptural imagery. The figure of Christ connects and merges with the imagery of the scriptural text or with interpretive imagery that has grown up around the text. This christological recentering can be seen most clearly in Romans 10:6–8 and 1 Corinthians 10:4 (10:1–21).

Christ and the Commandment of God

In the reference to Deuteronomy 30:12–14 in Romans 10:6–8, it is evident that Paul has substituted Christ for the commandment of God in the scriptural passage. The apostle introduces the citation with the words, "Do not say in your heart," found in both Deuteronomy 8:17 and 9:4. Following this injunction, Paul quotes selectively from Deuteronomy 30:12–14 (emphasis mine):

> But the righteousness that comes from faith says, "Do not say in your heart, 'Who will ascend into heaven?' " (that is, to bring Christ down) "or 'Who will descend into the abyss?' " (that is, to bring Christ up from the dead). But what does it *say*?
>
> > "The word is near you,
> > on your lips and in your heart"
>
> (that is, the word of faith that we proclaim).

The most conspicuous structural feature of Romans 10:6–8 is the threefold pattern of the text: (1) scriptural citation, (2) introduction to the exposition ("that is"), and (3) exposition. This form is repeated three times in these verses. In the interpretive remarks that Paul appends to the text of Deuteronomy, it is immediately apparent that Christ has become the referent of the text. In this way, Paul has transformed a text, which in its scriptural context is about the law, into a text about Christ.

In the context of Romans 9:30–10:21, verses 6–8 serve as a transition. Deuteronomy 30:12–14 is introduced as a text about righteousness by faith and the passage is used as part of the argument that Paul has developed in 9:30–10:5. In 10:8, however, the interpretation of Deuteronomy 30:14 focuses on the "word of faith" that is proclaimed. In 10:9–21, the discussion is no longer primarily about "faith" versus "works" but about proclamation, faith, and obedience. The "word" in Deuteronomy 30:14 is used by Paul to change the focus of the discussion; the "word" of the scriptural text relates to the "word of faith" of apostolic proclamation. And the "word of faith," for Paul, is about Jesus whom God raised from the dead.

From the perspective of Paul's conversation with scripture, the aspect of Romans 10:6–8 that is most intriguing is the manner in which Christ has been substituted for the "word" of God's command. Implicit in Paul's use of Deuteronomy 30:12–14 is the connection between Christ and the commandment of God. As a result of this connection,

Paul in his interpretive comments on the scriptural text replaces the
legal imagery with christological imagery. The discussion in Romans
9:30–10:8 displays a clear symbolic, indeed interpretive, link between
Christ and the commandment of God.

It is common for those who comment on Romans 10:6–8 to make
reference to the connection between Torah and wisdom in Jewish
tradition.[1] Without any doubt, the tendency toward the personifica-
tion of wisdom in Jewish language and imagery and the connection
between Torah and wisdom in this tradition can be compared to the
connection between Christ and the commandment of God in 10:6–8.
Perhaps the most striking text for comparison is Baruch 3:9–4:4. In
3:29–32a, the author writes concerning wisdom:

> Who has gone up into heaven, and taken her,
>   and brought her down from the clouds?
> Who has gone over the sea, and found her,
>   and will buy her for pure gold?
> No one knows the way to her
>   or is concerned about the path to her.
> But the one who knows all things knows her,
>   he found her by his understanding.

The writer in Baruch 3:9 calls upon Israel to hear the commandments
of life and to pay attention to wisdom, and in 4:1 wisdom is identified
as the book of the commandments of God and the law that exists into
eternity. In language that clearly reflects Deuteronomy 30:12–13 (Bar.
3:29–30), this author announces that God has brought wisdom to
Israel, and in Baruch wisdom is defined explicitly in terms of Torah.[2]
The significance of this text is that in the Jewish wisdom tradition not
only is wisdom identified as Torah, but also in a context in which a
reference to Deuteronomy 30:12–13 is included, God is portrayed as
having made wisdom accessible in Torah. In the giving of Torah, God
has given wisdom to Israel. The figurative language represented by
the terms "heaven" and "across the sea" serve to portray the hidden-
ness or inaccessibility that has been overcome in the giving of
wisdom/Torah.[3] Because the writer of Baruch affirms a connection

between wisdom and Torah, it follows naturally for him that Deuteronomy 30:12–13 refers to wisdom, though in the scriptural context it refers to the commandment of God.

In the Wisdom of Jesus Ben Sira, also called Sirach or the book of Ecclesiasticus, the imagery of personified wisdom in chapter 24 is even more striking than in Baruch. Wisdom is pictured as coming out of the mouth of God and covering the earth (24:2–3). She was created by God and was commanded to dwell in Jacob (24:8–9). In 24:5 Sirach writes: "Alone I compassed the vault of heaven and traversed the depths of the abyss." Later in the same chapter, in 24:23, it is announced that the things that have been written are the book of the law: "All this is the book of the covenant of the Most High God, the law that Moses commanded us." Sirach's wisdom teaching is grounded in the legal traditions of scripture. Not only does Sirach represent wisdom in personified terms, but the close connection in his theology between wisdom and the commandments of God allows him to portray wisdom as representing Torah.

This discussion illustrates that within Jewish tradition there was a tendency to view wisdom in personified terms, to allow wisdom to assume the character and role of Torah, and to apply to wisdom scriptural passages and language that in their scriptural contexts pertain to the commandments of God. In the interpretive comments that Paul appends to the three parts of the scriptural citation in Romans 10:6–8, the person of Christ functions similarly. In 9:30–10:8, Christ is portrayed in religious as well as personal terms; he is described as the *telos* ("end," "goal") of the law, and Deuteronomy 30:12–14 is understood as pertaining directly to him. In Paul's interpretation of this passage, the person of Christ assumes in a figurative way the place of God's commandment as represented in the scriptural text. The "word of faith" is near rather than the "word of the commandment."

Christ and the "Rock"

In 1 Corinthians 10:4 Paul writes: "For they drank from the spiritual rock that followed them, and the rock was Christ." It has long been recognized by students of Paul that 10:1–4 is related to certain Jewish traditions.[4] For our purposes only the salient features of these traditions and their scriptural background must be rehearsed. In Exodus 17:1–7, the people of Israel are said to be encamped at Rephidim, a place where there is no water for them to drink. Because of their thirst, the people grumble against Moses, and Moses calls out to God. God instructs Moses to strike the rock, whereupon water will flow from the rock. Having done this and received the water, Moses names the place Massah ("proof") and Meribah ("contention") because of the people's contentious demand for proof of God's presence with them.

A related story is recorded in Numbers 20:1–13. On this occasion, the people of Israel are at Kadesh, but once again they are without water. Moses is instructed to tell the rock to bring forth water. He strikes the rock with his rod and water comes forth; in the scriptural text it is announced that these are the waters of Meribah. That the waters from the rock at both Rephidim and Kadesh are called Meribah has apparently suggested to some people within later tradition that water from the same rock is present in both places:[5] "And so the well which was with the Israelites in the wilderness was a rock. . . . Wherever the Israelites would encamp, it made camp with them."[6] The image of the well or water following Israel in the wilderness appears to stem from Numbers 21:16–18:

> From there they continued to Beer; that is the well of which the LORD said to Moses, "Gather the people together, and I will give them water." Then Israel sang this song:
>
> > "Spring up, O well—Sing to it!—
> > the well that the leaders sank,
> > that the nobles of the people dug,
> > with the scepter, with the staff."[7]

And in Midrash Rabbah (a rabbinic Jewish biblical interpretation) on Numbers 1:1, it is written:

> And the well was due to the merit of Miriam. For what does scripture say? "And Miriam died there, and was buried there." And what is written

after that? "And there was no water for the congregation." How was the well constructed? It was rock-shaped like a bee-hive, and wherever they journeyed it rolled along and came with them. When the standards (under which the tribes journeyed) halted and the tabernacle was set up, that same rock would come and settle down in the court of the Tent of Meeting and the princes would come and stand upon it and say, "rise up, O well," and it would rise.[8]

It is evident from these texts that there are a number of different elements that can be identified in this tradition: (1) the rock that brings forth water, (2) the well that brings forth water, (3) the rock that follows the people, and (4) the stream of water that follows the people.[9] For our purposes, the one feature that must be noted is the connection between the rock and the well.[10] The Targum of Onkelos, an Aramaic biblical translation of Numbers 21:16–20, implies that the well was also present on the occasion recounted in Numbers 20:1–13.[11] According to Midrash Rabbah on Numbers 1:1, the connection is made quite directly between the well and the "rock shaped like a bee-hive." Hence, there is no doubt that there was a link between the rock and the well in the development of this tradition, and there is no reason to suppose that this connection did not emerge early in the development of the interpretive process. At least, it is evident from 1 Corinthians 10:4 that Paul was familiar with the tradition of the "following" rock that brought forth water to Israel.

The final, and perhaps most crucial, link in this discussion is supplied by the Damascus Rule, found among the Dead Sea Scrolls. In 6:3–4 it is written: "And they dug the well: 'the well which the princes dug, which the nobles of the people delved with the stave.' The well is the law." Not only is Numbers 21:18 quoted, but the well is explicitly identified as the law. This demonstrates that the sectarian community had equated the well with the law and had related Numbers 21:18 to the task of Torah interpretation. While it cannot be established with certainty that this identification was known widely beyond the confines of the Dead Sea community, there are indications that suggest that it was. We know that Philo of Alexandria, roughly a contemporary of

Paul, equated the "rock" with the wisdom of God.[12] In the light of the connection between the "rock" and the "well" and between Torah and wisdom, it is possible, if not probable, that there was also a link between the "well" and the Torah in the traditions that were available to Philo.

It is also noteworthy that in Deuteronomy 1:5 it says: "Moses undertook to expound this law." The Hebrew word that is here translated "to expound" is probably a cognate of the Hebrew word meaning "well." It is interesting to speculate that by the time Deuteronomy was written there was already a verbal connection between the act of explaining Torah and the image of the "well." As the ancient Israelites were sustained and nourished by the life-giving water of the "well" that followed them in the desert, so now the people of God are given sustenance and life by that which flows from the Torah. The evidence suggests that there was within Israel a fairly widespread identification of Torah with the desert "well," and, as we have seen, the connection between the "well" and the "rock" was firmly established. Thus, the connection between Torah and the "rock" would certainly have been a natural association.

Therefore, it is distinctly possible that the apostle was aware of a figurative association between the "rock" and Torah. If this is in fact the case, it may be argued that Paul's identification of the "rock" as Christ also reflects an association between the law and Christ, as is evident in Romans 10:6–8. It must be emphasized that the language and imagery of 1 Corinthians 10:1–4 is related most directly to the Exodus, baptism, and the Eucharist, but this does not preclude the possibility that Paul was aware of a connection between the "rock," the "well," and Torah, and that Christ as the source of spiritual drink assumed in a figurative sense the role of the Torah by being identified with the "rock." Therefore, the symbolic and interpretive linking of Christ with the law and legal imagery is not only found in Romans 10:6–8 but also in 1 Corinthians 10:4. Unlike Romans 10:6–8, however, there is an identification or equation expressed in figurative language in 1 Corinthians 10:4: ". . . the rock was Christ."

What Romans 10:6–8 and 1 Corinthians 10:4 indicate is that Paul has associated the figure of Christ with a scriptural concept (commandment of God) or object (rock) and has used the scriptural language and imagery to illustrate what he considers to be a contemporary reality; namely, that Christ is the manifestation of the divine presence and activity. In neither of these texts does he elaborate extensively his messianic understanding. He appears to be satisfied with drawing on the scriptural imagery, using this imagery to develop his argument, and in this way applying the scriptural material to his own circumstance in the early church. In both cases, Christology plays an important but supporting role in a larger discussion.

Christ and Wisdom

In the foregoing discussion, we have noticed that passages from the Jewish wisdom tradition, or at least pertaining to wisdom, have surfaced on more than one occasion. The connection between Torah and wisdom has also been documented. Torah as the revelation of God is indeed the wisdom of God made known to the chosen people. The wisdom tradition may have had an international flavor in its inception in Israel, and it may have only gradually been absorbed into the covenantal traditions of the people of God. But that it was incorporated into the legal traditions of Israel there can be no doubt. The gift of Torah was the manifestation of divine Wisdom.

It should come as no surprise that Paul explicitly identifies Christ as the "power" and "wisdom" of God in 1 Corinthians 1:24 and as "our wisdom" in 1:30. While the apostle does not develop these assertions or summon scriptural support for them, they are in a context (1:18–3:23) in which biblical material is cited no less than six times. If Christ is linked symbolically with Torah, it follows naturally for Paul, the Jew, to assume that Christ is also the wisdom of God. Christ brings to expression God's wisdom that has now been revealed apart from the law. First Corinthians 1:18–3:23, to be sure, contains a discussion focused on the contrast between wisdom and folly, the preaching of the cross and the wisdom of this world, but as Paul uses these words and phrases, he acknowledges that Christ, the wisdom of God, has also been made "our" righteousness, sanctification, and redemption. Thus, Paul's use of wisdom is directly related to his understanding of God's saving purposes. It also illustrates another dimension of the way in which the apostle has utilized the Torah/wisdom traditions of his people to establish Christ as God's revelation, God's gift to God's people.

Proverbs 3:19 states: "The Lord by wisdom founded the earth." In 8:30, the writer of Proverbs concludes a description of wisdom's creation by noting wisdom's presence alongside the creator:

> Then I was beside him, like a master worker [or: little child];
> and I was daily his delight,
>   rejoicing before him always.

The apostle Paul does not allow his Christology to undermine the monotheistic conviction of Judaism, but he does picture Christ as the agent of God in creation. In 1 Corinthians 8:6, Paul writes: "Yet for us there is one God, the Father, from whom are all things and for whom we exist, and one Lord, Jesus Christ, through whom are all things and through whom we exist." If wisdom is the agent of creation or at least the handmaiden of the creator for the writer of Proverbs, it is clear that for Paul Christ has assumed this role. Christ, the wisdom of God, is the agent through whom God has brought into being all things. In Colossians 1:15–16 we also read: "He is the image of the invisible God, the firstborn of all creation; for in him all things in heaven and on earth were created." Once again, the role often attributed to wisdom in the Jewish wisdom tradition is taken over by Christ. This makes sense if, as Paul assumes, Christ is the wisdom of God. It follows quite directly from the presupposition that he is the manifestation of God's wisdom and the expression of divine revelation. Christ is the image of God, the firstborn of creation. Wisdom and its association with Torah give Paul a conceptual context for understanding Christ as the expression of divine activity and the agent of God in creation.

Conclusion

It is clear that Paul shifts the Jewish conceptual system. Christ and what ensues from him (for example, the church) are theologically central in Paul's symbolic worldview. As a result, the symbolic world of the scriptural text begins to reflect the christological symbolism of the apostle's view of divine activity. Interpretively, the sacred text and the christological context have fused to produce a new set of concepts and images, which in turn extend the meaning of the text. In this manner, the interpretive cycle is continued.

This christological centering of the divine drama is finally what makes Pauline Christianity and the classical Christian "story" distinctive. The "word of faith" has come near in proclamation, not the commandment of God. Christ, not the law, is the "well-spring" of divine nourishment. Christ, not Torah, is the Wisdom of God. Indeed, Christ is the agent of God in creation. The distinctively Pauline account of divine activity is arranged symbolically around the figure of Christ, even though Paul in his epistles does not feel compelled to argue on the basis of scripture for the messiahship of Jesus. In that sense, the significance of Christ is assumed. He is at the heart of the Pauline religious system.

Epilogue

One of the significant advances in biblical studies has been the realization, drawn largely from social theory, that "knowing" as related to historical and literary matters is socially conditioned and in large measure socially determined. This kind of "knowing" is governed and made possible by a social network of symbols, devices, and relationships that make knowledge and communication possible. Indeed, the act of "knowing" itself is probably not possible apart from a complex array of social arrangements. Moreover, the "knower" himself or herself is always part of a network of social relationships that govern his or her ability to know. In other words, the "knower" and the "known" are both part of a social world and in some cases even part of the same social world. They are socially rooted and cannot finally be separated from their social contexts.[1]

These insights are closely related to the conversation model of interpretation. The contexts of both the biblical text and the interpreter are interlaced with a network of social symbols and relationships. Though I have argued that the modern critical interpreter of scripture ought to seek the context of the biblical text, it is certainly clear by now that interpretation in fact involves the merging and blending of two quite separate voices and their respective contexts, those of the text and the interpreter. The manner in which this merging and blending takes place and the proportional balance between the two may vary, but in the process of textual interpretation the voice and context of the interpreter and the voice and context of the text come into some form of relationship or symbolic alignment. At the point where this happens, the biblical text is determined by the interpreter to have meaning or to make sense.

The claims that Paul makes about his biblical text, however, are not simply claims about the meaning of a literary text. They are often claims about divine purpose and reality. For Paul, the biblical text is the revelation of God. It is the *sacred* text. In that sense, it is not merely a written text to be apprehended or understood. It is an arena for discovering God's purpose and intention. The biblical text is dynamic and generative. It transcends the mere letters of the text and becomes a conduit for the word of God. Thus, Paul's use of biblical texts is intimately tied up with his own religious experience and with his reflection on that experience, namely his theology. This religious experience casts new light on the texts of scripture, and it allows Paul to uncover new insights into the nature of divine reality and the structure of redemption. Out of this complex set of religious and theological circumstances emerge the claims that Paul makes about the meaning of scripture. In Paul's New Testament epistles, we are given only a glimpse into the character of this interpretive process, but, as we have now seen, several significant observations can nevertheless be gleaned from the literary legacy Paul has left to us.

Throughout these pages I have argued that Paul's hermeneutic is inseparable from his Christology, even though he does not by and large elaborate his Christology with the aid of scriptural material. To be sure, Paul's interpretation of biblical texts emerges from a social context and is directed toward communities of faith, fledgling churches. In that sense, Richard Hays is correct. Paul's use of scripture in the epistles is ecclesiological.[2] To put it succinctly, Paul is concerned about the common life and unity of a church composed of both Jews and Gentiles, and it is to that end that he writes his epistles. But Christology in no sense is removed from that process. The figure of Christ and the symbols associated with Christ are at the very heart of Paul's experience on the Damascus road and the subsequent religious transformation that ensued from that experience. The belief that Christ is the agent of divine redemption and that he has now been revealed shapes Paul's worldview and his religious context. Indeed, Christ becomes part of the network of presuppositions and symbols that govern Paul's reading of scripture. These presuppositions in turn govern the perceptions and conclusions that Paul claims to derive from the texts of scripture. The implications of this observation are anything but trivial, for they suggest that to understand the implications of Paul's use of scripture one must also understand something of the apostle's religious and theological context. In doing that, the modern interpreter is thrust directly into the complexity of Paul's theological legacy.

It is also clear from this discussion that the social context for biblical interpretation is evolutionary in character. The church's corporate life and theology, for example, are constantly being made and remade. It is true that the church as a community of believers may often make absolute claims for its theology or proclamation, but even these claims and their formulation are conditioned by the social environment of the community that makes them. Even if we are not prepared to reduce all of the church's theological claims to a series of social factors, it is virtually impossible to deny the social character of religion and the developmental nature of its theological reflection, including the interpretation of its sacred texts.

To many, this observation may seem obvious, but it is important because it affects the way we understand the function of religion, the Christian faith, and theology in a pluralistic and rapidly changing world. Change is the prevailing order of things in much of the modern church. It can be resisted, and it can be lamented. But it cannot be stopped. Thus, I would argue, the role of the church is to be active and not simply descriptive. It is to be active in shaping its future evolutionary course and not passive in the face of unprecedented social change. In this process, the heritage of the church is not discounted but is part of the very substance of theological reflection, as well as a point of reference in an uncertain world. In this way, the historical and theological heritage of the church enables the community of faith to approach the future with confidence, without being constrained by inappropriate conceptions and outmoded theologies. For the church to resist or ignore this developmental process seems to me to be the surest route to irrelevance.

This, of course, begs the question of Christianity's eternal and essential truths. Are there any? If so, what are they and how are they preserved? Most Christians would agree that there are elements in

Christianity that are nonnegotiable in the church's process of renewal and reformulation. But, I would argue, these determinations are always made in context, and they are made relative to a "circle of plausibility." Different individuals and groups within Christianity will thus disagree about the essentials of their religion and the way these essentials are to be formulated.

For example, the claim that Jesus is Lord (or the Christ) is a tenet of Christianity. Apart from this claim, the religion appears to lose its coherence and internal logic. People outside Christianity will certainly not subscribe to this claim, but for Christians this is a conspicuous feature of their religion and theology. However, the meaning and significance of the assertion that Jesus is Lord is subject (has been subject) to widely varying interpretations among people all claiming to be within the Christian community. In short, the statement that Jesus is Lord is a proposition that is subject to its own interpretation. From this claim about Jesus, the process of christological development was put into motion and continues to the present day. It has spawned its own elaboration and revision. The truth claims that are made on behalf of Christianity are themselves organically linked to the communities that produce them and the traditions that follow from them. These truth claims never exist apart from a set of social and historical circumstances.

In that social and historical matrix, the Bible itself functions as a foundational document for the Christian community. It is turned to for guidance, nourishment, and instruction. What makes the Bible foundational is that it is deemed to be authoritative and that subsequent communities of faith are compelled to return to it again and again to discover its word of divine address. Beyond the simple cultural influence of the Bible, the Christian community through worship and study finds in the scriptures clues to its identity and its heritage, as well as a vocabulary to describe its religious experience and sustain its spiritual life. Through ongoing conversation with the scriptures, the Christian community develops its theology and its liturgical life. It conforms its corporate life to the Bible, even as the Bible itself is conformed to the common life of the community. The mechanism for this interchange is hermeneutics. At its best, this process involves not only interpretation of the biblical text but also interpretation of the interpreter's social and historical context.

In this process, Pauline texts become meaningful when the modern reader's world begins to overlap the world of the text or is brought into some kind of juxtaposition with it. Only to the extent that this overlap or juxtaposition occurs will the Pauline text come to be meaningful and understandable to the modern reader. When this overlap or juxtaposition cannot or will not be made, the text remains not only remote but in many ways incomprehensible. Hence, the job of the Pauline interpreter is to seek ways for this conceptual overlap or alignment to take place. Without this effort, any residual authority of the Pauline texts (biblical texts) begins to erode, until the interpretive conversation eventually ceases. In this event, the epistles are no longer considered important, meaningful, or interesting enough to warrant further dialogue.

Using the symbolism associated with Abraham, Israel, Adam, and Torah, I have sought to illustrate four rather interesting examples of Pauline conversations with biblical texts. But beyond this, I have also suggested ways that Paul's texts might in turn begin to inform our own conversations. The universal gospel of inclusion and the oneness of the church have important implications for the way the modern community of faith addresses the world and strives for unity. Perhaps it is appropriate once again for the Christian community to emphasize with renewed urgency the universal and inclusive character of God's good news in which social, racial, and gender distinctions are finally rendered null.

In this regard, Paul is an example for the modern church. He moves beyond his own sectarianism to bring the universal message of Christ to a world that in many ways is alien to it. He cannot simply be a transmitter of tradition. He must formulate, indeed create, a theology and a religious posture that can communicate to people in the Roman world of his time. The church today is confronted with issues that require it also to be more than a conduit for the received tradition. The church is called upon to explore unexplored theological issues and problems. It is required to do theology afresh and not merely repeat the well-worn theological maxims of the past. Far from allowing

Christian people of today to ignore the traditions of the past, however, the demands of our day make it imperative that we know well the church's heritage so that we can use it constructively in forging the theologies of the future. The universal implication of the Pauline gospel is a constant reminder to the church to move beyond itself and its narrow institutional concerns. The universal character of the gospel is finally the most promising antidote to religious exclusivism and to the institutionalization of the church. But perhaps above all, the church is called upon to speak to a rapidly changing world that often seems both alien to traditional formulations of the gospel message and also alienated from it by the example of the church. It is precisely on this theological frontier that the church today is called to do its work and interpret its scriptures.

It is certainly not novel in the post-Holocaust world to call for a renewed understanding of the church's relationship to Judaism and the Jewish people. But it may be somewhat ironic to suggest that Paul assist us in that effort. He has been considered an apostate by Jews and a refugee from the burdens of Torah by Christians. But Paul struggled without fail to hold the church and Israel together. He could not abandon Israel or the Jewish people. That would have threatened the very social and theological unity that he sought to preserve in the church. Hence, in the modern church's struggle against anti-Judaism, Paul's argument for God's faithfulness to the covenant and for the incorporation of Gentile Christianity into the Israelite rootstock sounds important theological themes.

Life in the church is in many ways dialectical. Opposites are juxtaposed as a way of ordering Christian experience. One paradigm for this dialectical expression of Christian existence is the Adam/Christ typology in Romans 5. For Paul, the structure of existence is defined by the symbolic juxtaposition of Adam and Christ. They represent symbolic categories that serve to order the way life in Christ and life apart from Christ are perceived. The dialectic in Romans 5 is a lens through which Paul views Christian existence. It is not primarily a historical description of original sin. In the Christian symbolic network, Adam and Christ serve as categories around which to organize and interpret the experience of grace and the reality of death.

Finally, I have illustrated the way Paul recenters his religious system christologically. At the heart of the Pauline "story" of redemption stands the symbolic figure of Christ. Stemming from his own experience on the Damascus road, Christ becomes a, if not the, prominent symbol in Paul's religious system. The figure of Christ and what he represents become for Paul a cluster of symbols around which other religious symbols are arranged and interpreted. Christ, not the law, is the "well-spring" of divine nourishment. Christ, not Torah, is the wisdom of God. Christ is both the agent of creation and the agent of redemption. Christ is Lord.

Notes

Prologue

1. Richard B. Hays, *Echoes of Scripture in the Letters of Paul* (New Haven, Conn.: Yale University Press, 1989).

2. See in English, for example, E. Earle Ellis, *Paul's Use of the Old Testament* (Grand Rapids: Wm. B. Eerdmans Publishing Co., 1957). Compare also the end notes in Hays's book, *Echoes of Scripture,* for other titles, including works in German and French.

3. For a recent discussion of some of these issues, see D. Moody Smith, "The Pauline Literature," in *It Is Written: Scripture Citing Scripture— Essays in Honour of Barnabas Lindars,* ed. D. A. Carson and H. G. M. Williamson (Cambridge: Cambridge University Press, 1988), 276–288.

I. Ancient Text, Modern Book

1. See, for example, Anthony C. Thiselton, *The Two Horizons* (Grand Rapids: Wm. B. Eerdmans Publishing Co., 1980), 293–326, and C. René Padilla, "The Interpreted Word: Reflections on Contextual Hermeneutics" in *A Guide to Contemporary Hermeneutics: Major Trends in Biblical Interpretation,* ed. Donald K. McKim (Grand Rapids: Wm. B. Eerdmans Publishing Co., 1986), 297–308. I resist uses of the Bible that refuse to take seriously the integrity (historical/literary) of the biblical text. In extreme forms of "reader-oriented" uses of literary material, the text often appears to be little more than a pretext. One wonders if the text itself does not become superfluous.

2. Compare the approach of Richard B. Hays, *Echoes of Scripture* (New Haven, Conn.: Yale University Press, 1989), 1–33.

II. A Hebrew Born of Hebrews

1. E. P. Sanders, *Paul and Palestinian Judaism: A Comparison of Patterns of Religion* (Philadelphia: Fortress Press, 1977), 2–4.

2. Ibid., 4–6.

3. Ibid., 7–9.

4. Ibid., 8. See J. Christiaan Beker, *Paul the Apostle: The Triumph of God in Life and Thought* (Edinburgh: T. & T. Clark, 1980), 16–19.

5. Sanders, *Paul and Palestinian Judaism*, 549.

6. Ibid., 431–442, and Krister Stendahl, "The Apostle Paul and the Introspective Conscience of the West," in *Paul Among Jews and Gentiles* (Philadelphia: Fortress Press, 1976), 78–96.

7. James Aageson, "Typology, Correspondence, and the Application of Scripture in Romans 9–11," *Journal for the Study of the New Testament* 31 (1987): 51–72.

8. Beker, *Paul the Apostle*, 288.

9. Alan F. Segal, *Rebecca's Children: Judaism and Christianity in the Roman World* (Cambridge, Mass.: Harvard University Press, 1986), 64–67.

10. Ibid., 64.

11. Ibid., 65.

12. Donald Juel, *Messianic Exegesis: Christological Interpretation of the Old Testament in Early Christianity* (Philadelphia: Fortress Press, 1988), 11.

13. Ibid., 13.

14. Stendahl, "Introspective Conscience," 78–96.

15. Sanders, *Paul and Palestinian Judaism,* 442–447.

16. See below, pp. 80–87.

17. See the discussion by David J. Lull, " 'The Law Was Our Pedagogue': A Study in Galatians 3:19–25," *Journal of Biblical Literature* 105 (1986): 482–486.

18. It has been argued that there is development in Paul's thought from Galatians to Romans. See Hans Hübner, *Law in Paul's Thought,* trans. James C. G. Greig (Edinburgh: T. & T. Clark, 1984), 1–7.

19. See Paul J. Achtemeier, " 'Some Things in Them Hard to Understand': Reflections on an Approach to Paul," *Interpretation* 38 (1984): 263–267.

20. See also Rom. 13:9; Matt. 22:34–40; Mark 12:28–34; and James 2:8.

21. The words "revelation" and "to reveal" together appear twenty-six times in the Pauline letters.

22. Compare Acts 9:1–22; 22:1–16; 26:12–18.

23. See, for example, Lloyd Gaston, *Paul and Torah* (Vancouver: University of British Columbia, 1987), 151–168; Richard B. Hays, *Echoes of Scripture* (New Haven, Conn.: Yale University Press, 1989), 122–125; Stephen Westerholm, "Letter and Spirit: The Foundation of Pauline Ethics," *New Testament Studies* 30 (1984): 229–248; and Ernst Käsemann, "The Spirit and the Letter," in *Perspectives on Paul,* trans. Margaret Kohl (Philadelphia: Fortress Press, 1971), 138–166.

24. Exodus 34:29–35 is the scriptural material upon which the discussion in 2 Cor. 3:7–18 is based. It appears that the translation of 2 Cor.

3:16 included in the text of the Revised English Bible ("whenever he turns to the Lord the veil is removed") tends to obscure the contemporary character of what Paul is saying and that the translation of the New Revised Standard Version should be adopted (". . . but when one turns to the Lord, the veil is removed"). It would seem that the expression "to this day" (v.15) governs the temporal sense of the text. Paul is playing on the image of "turning" as a way to describe a present reality.

25. Hays, *Echoes of Scripture*, 130.

26. Ibid., 130.

27. E. Earle Ellis, *Paul's Use of the Old Testament* (Grand Rapids: Wm. B. Eerdmans Publishing Co., 1957), 27.

28. Hays, *Echoes of Scripture*, 151.

29. Ibid., 133–140. Compare the rather curious statement in 2 Cor. 3:17 that the Lord is the Spirit. For Paul, there is clearly a connection between belief in the Lord, the Spirit, and freedom.

30. See Ulrich Wilckens, *Der Brief an die Römer,* Evangelisch-Katholischer Kommentar, 3 vols. (Zurich: Benziger Verlag; Neukirchen-Vluyn: Neukirchener Verlag, 1978–1982), 1:63–64.

31. Jesus, the Messiah and gospel of God, was promised beforehand in the Holy Scriptures. Paul makes this claim, but he neither substantiates it nor gives the biblical texts that he has in mind. Paul did not feel compelled to substantiate his remarks in Rom. 1:1–7 exegetically for the tradition apparently carried sufficient authority to be accepted without further elaboration. A simple reference was all that was necessary to bring to mind the point that Paul wanted to make.

32. For other New Testament examples in which the "prophets" are used with the "law" to refer to the scriptures see Matt. 5:17; 7:12; 11:13; 22:40; Luke 16:16; 24:44; John 1:45; Acts 13:15; 24:14; and 28:23.

33. See Hans Conzelmann, *1 Corinthians,* trans. James W. Leitch, Hermeneia (Philadelphia: Fortress Press, 1975), 251–256, and "On the Analysis of the Confessional Formula in I Corinthians 15:3–5," *Interpretation* 20 (1966): 15–25; and John Kloppenborg, "An Analysis of the Pre-Pauline Formula I Cor. 15:3b–5 in Light of Some Recent Literature," *Catholic Biblical Quarterly* 40 (1978): 351–367.

34. Richard B. Hays underscores this point forcefully, *Echoes of Scripture,* especially 84–87. However, to say that Paul does not in the main argue or develop his Christology on the basis of scriptural texts is not the same as saying that he does not use scripture christologically.

35. See Rom. 9:33; 10:6–8; 11:26; 15:9–12; 1 Cor. 15:25–27; Gal. 3:13–16.

36. Sanders, *Paul and Palestinian Judaism,* 442–447. See also John Gager's effort to reinterpret Paul, *The Origins of Anti-Semitism: Attitudes Toward Judaism in Pagan and Christian Antiquity* (New York: Oxford University Press, 1985), 193–264.

37. See Jeffrey S. Siker, *Disinheriting the Jews: Abraham in Early Christian Controversy* (Louisville, Ky.: Westminster/John Knox Press, 1991), 28–76, 185–198.

38. See below, pp. 78–81.

39. Segal, *Rebecca's Children,* 1. See also Jacob Neusner, *From Testament to Torah: An Introduction to Judaism in Its Formative Age* (Englewood Cliffs, N.J.: Prentice-Hall, 1988), xiii–xviii.

III. Testified to by the Law and the Prophets

1. See, for example, 1 Cor. 1:18–25 and Gal. 3:6–14.

2. See, for example, Rom. 15:3; 1 Cor. 9:9–10; 14:21.

3. Compare Rom. 11:2–4 in which Paul cites and applies 1 Kings 19:10 and 18.

4. Compare 1 Cor. 4:6–7.

5. Anthony Tyrrell Hanson, *Studies in Paul's Technique and Theology* (London: SPCK, 1974), 159–168.

6. Ernest De Witt Burton, *A Critical and Exegetical Commentary on the Epistle to the Galatians,* International Critical Commentary (Edinburgh: T. & T. Clark, 1921), 253–255.

7. Ibid., 256.

8. Ibid., 254.

9. Ibid.

10. Hans Dieter Betz, *Galatians: A Commentary on Paul's Letter to the Churches in Galatia,* Hermeneia (Philadelphia: Fortress Press, 1979), 243.

11. Ibid., 254.

12. This aspect of Paul's use of scripture in Romans 9–11 has been worked out in detail in my article, "Scripture and Structure in the Development of the Argument in Romans 9–11," *Catholic Biblical Quarterly* 48 (April 1986): 265–289.

13. Compare Rom. 11:13–14.

14. Because we are looking at Paul's conversation with scripture and because we are looking at this aspect of Paul's work from a largely Jewish point of view, it is not necessary for us to examine Greek rhetorical patterns in the epistles. Greek rhetoric is, however, another element in the Pauline literature. See George Kennedy, *New Testament Interpretation Through Rhetorical Criticism,* Studies in Religion (Chapel Hill, N.C.: University of North Carolina Press, 1984), and Stanley

Kent Stowers, *The Diatribe and Paul's Letter to the Romans,* SBL Dissertation Series (Chico, Calif.: Scholars Press, 1981).

15. Compare, for example, Barnabas Lindars, *New Testament Apologetic: The Doctrinal Significance of the Old Testament Quotations* (London: SCM Press, 1961).

16. For example, Rendel Harris, *Testimonies,* 2 vols. (Cambridge: Cambridge University Press, 1916 and 1920), passim; C. H. Dodd, *According to the Scriptures: The Sub-Structure of New Testament Theology* (London: James Nisbet & Co., 1952), 41–43; Lindars, *New Testament Apologetic,* 169–181; and Edward Gordon Selwyn, *The First Epistle of St. Peter* (London: Macmillan & Co., 1946), 268–277.

17. For a reconstruction of the way the "stone" passages were used in the early church, see Lindars, *New Testament Apologetic,* 169–186.

18. C. E. B. Cranfield argues that the Jews pursued the law that was given to Israel to bring her to righteousness but pursued it in the wrong way; see "Some Notes on Romans 9:30–33," in *Jesus und Paulus,* ed. E. Earle Ellis and Erich Grässer (Göttingen: Vandenhoeck & Ruprecht, 1975), 35–43.

19. C. K. Barrett, "Romans 9:30–10:21: Fall and Responsibility of Israel," *Essays on Paul* (London: SPCK, 1982), 144.

20. To argue that the pronoun "him" in Rom. 10:11 refers to God and not specifically to Christ is to ignore the christological nature of Paul's argument in 10:6–9 and 10:14–17. If this pronoun were to refer to God in 10:11, it would also mean that the same pronoun must refer to God in 9:33. This is not impossible, but the result of this interpretation would mean that the "stone" and the pronoun "him" would necessarily refer to different things in the same verse (9:33), which seems rather unlikely in light of the content of the passage.

21. See also 1 Peter 2:22 (Isa. 53:9); 2:24 (Isa. 53:4, 5, 12); and 2:25 (Isa. 53:6).

IV. Abraham and the Gospel of Inclusion

1. See the discussion above regarding Rom. 1:1–7 and 3:21–26, pp. 35–36. Paul, of course, does use the word "promise," but he does not explicitly refer to the fulfillment of the biblical words. However, the concept of fulfillment is clearly implied.

2. See Matt. 1:1.

3. See the discussions by E. A. Speiser, *Genesis: Introduction, Translation, and Notes*, Anchor Bible (Garden City, N. Y.: Doubleday & Co., 1964), 120–121, and John Van Seters, "The Problem of Childlessness in Near Eastern Law and the Patriarchs of Israel," *Journal of Biblical Literature* 87 (December 1968): 405–408.

4. See the discussion in E. P. Sanders, *Paul, the Law, and the Jewish People* (Philadelphia: Fortress Press, 1983), 13–14, note 18.

5. See the discussion on Gal. 3:6–8 above, p. 37. Note that in the quotation of Genesis 12:3 Paul cites the word *ethnē* ("Gentiles/nations") instead of the word *phylē* ("families"), which is used in the Greek versions.

6. For a general discussion of the conflict in Galatia, see Werner Georg Kümmel, *Introduction to the New Testament*, rev. ed., trans. Howard Clark Kee (Nashville: Abingdon Press, 1975), 299–300.

7. David J. Lull, " 'The Law Was Our Pedagogue': A Study in Galatians 3:19–25," *Journal of Biblical Literature* 105 (September 1986): 481–486.

8. The term *gezerah shawah* means literally "equal laws," but it came to apply to the comparison of similar verbal expressions. If the same or similar words appear in two texts, the law that applies in one of them applies also to the other.

9. Krister Stendahl, "Paul and the Introspective Conscience of the West," in *Paul Among Jews and Gentiles* (Philadelphia: Fortress Press, 1976), 78–96.

10. Ibid. See also E. P. Sanders, *Paul and Palestinian Judaism* (Philadelphia: Fortress Press, 1977), 1–59.

V. Israel, the Rootstock of the Church

1. See my article entitled "Scripture and Structure in the Development of the Argument in Romans 9–11," *Catholic Biblical Quarterly* 48 (April 1986): 265–289.

2. See my discussion in "Typology, Correspondence, and the Application of Scripture in Romans 9–11," *Journal for the Study of the New Testament* 31 (1987): 54–56. Contrast Bruce W. Longenecker, "Different Answers to Different Issues: Israel, the Gentiles and Salvation History in Romans 9–11," *Journal for the Study of the New Testament* 36 (1989): 95–98.

3. Aageson, "Typology, Correspondence, and the Application of Scripture in Romans 9–11," 54–56.

4. Géza Vermès, *The Dead Sea Scrolls in English,* 2nd ed. (Harmondsworth, Middlesex: Penguin Books, 1975), 100.

5. See *2 Baruch* 40:2; *1 Enoch* 83:8; 90:30; *Sibylline Oracles* 5:384; 2 Esdras 9:7–8; 12:34; and 13:48.

6. This text appears in the context of Sirach's praise of Israel's patriarchs and heroes.

7. Vermès, *The Dead Sea Scrolls in English,* 169.

8. Ibid., 142.

9. See the discussion by C. E. B. Cranfield, *A Critical and Exegetical Commentary on the Epistle to the Romans* (Edinburgh: T. & T. Clark, 1975, 1979), 2:504–510.

10. See pp. 118–121.

11. See Aageson, "Typology, Correspondence, and the Application of Scripture in Romans 9–11," 71–72, note 56.

12. Compare the Mishnah, tractate *Sanhedrin* 10:1.

13. See, for example, Jacob Neusner, *From Testament to Torah* (Englewood Cliffs, N.J.: Prentice-Hall, 1988), 66–120.

VI. Adam and Christ

1. Elaine Pagels, *Adam, Eve, and the Serpent* (New York: Random House, 1988), 109 and 143.

2. K. J. Woollcombe, "The Biblical Origins and Patristic Development of Typology," in *Essays on Typology* (London: SCM, 1957), 60–65. Compare also the use of *typos* in Rom. 6:17; 1 Cor. 10:6 (10:11); Phil. 3:17; and 1 Thess. 1:7.

3. J. A. T. Robinson, *The Body: A Study of Pauline Theology*, Studies in Biblical Theology, no. 5 (Chicago: Henry Regnery Co., 1952), 35. See also Robin Scroggs, *The Last Adam: A Study in Pauline Anthropology* (Philadelphia: Fortress Press, 1966), 81. Scroggs accepts Robinson's suggestion.

4. Nils Alstrup Dahl, "The Argument in Rom. 5:12–21," in *Studies in Paul: Theology for the Early Christian Mission* (Minneapolis: Augsburg Publishing House, 1977), 90.

5. See the discussion by Karl Barth in *Christ and Adam: Man and Humanity in Romans 5*, trans. T. A. Smail (New York: Macmillan Co., 1957), 57–58.

6. The first principle of interpretation attributed to the Jewish rabbi Hillel and one that is encountered frequently in Jewish literature is referred to as *Qal Wahomer*. In this form of argumentation, it is asserted that that which applies in a case of lesser importance will be valid also in a case of greater importance. The primary requirement of

this manner of reasoning is that the initial element (Adam in this case) have some claim to being authoritative or to being accepted as true by the readers or hearers. Once this is established, the argument can be developed on the basis of an underlying connection between the two elements.

7. See Rudolf Bultmann, *The Old and New Man: In the Letters of Paul*, trans. Keith R. Crim (Richmond: John Knox Press, 1967), 64–65.

8. James D. G. Dunn, *Christology in the Making: A New Testament Inquiry into the Origins of the Doctrine of the Incarnation* (Philadelphia: Westminster Press, 1980), 105–107. See also Dunn's discussion of Adam and the plight of humanity in Rom. 1:18–25; 3:23; 7:7–11; and 8:19–23.

9. Ibid., 100. If the earthly man/heavenly man tradition was known to Paul, Christ then has been identified as this mythic heavenly figure. The heavenly man category has simply been applied to Christ.

10. See 1 Cor. 15:3–11.

11. For a discussion of the role of Psalms 8 and 110 in the Christology of 1 Corinthians 15, see Dunn, *Christology*, 108–111.

VII. Torah, Wisdom, and Christ

1. See, for example, Ernst Käsemann, *Commentary on Romans*, trans. Geoffrey W. Bromiley (London: SCM, 1980), 289; M. Jack Suggs, " 'The Word Is Near You': Romans 10:6–10 Within the Purpose of the Letter," in *Christian History and Interpretation*, ed. W. R. Farmer, C. F. D. Moule, and R. R. Niebuhr (Cambridge: Cambridge University Press, 1967), 305–312; and W. D. Davies, *Paul and Rabbinic Judaism: Some Rabbinic Elements in Pauline Theology* (London: SPCK, 1948), 153–154.

2. Suggs, " 'The Word Is Near You,' " 305–312. Compare Bar. 3:36 and Rom. 9:5, 13, and 11:28.

3. Compare the language and imagery in Prov. 30:3–4; Sir. 24:5; Eccl. 7:23–24; Job 28:12–14; and Rom. 11:33. Davies's comment that Bar. 3:29ff. refers to the "undiscoverability of wisdom" is technically correct, but in light of 3:35–4:4 it is evident that the inaccessibility of wisdom has been overcome by God (Davies, *Paul and Rabbinic Judaism*, 154).

4. As long ago as 1889, S. R. Driver addressed the issue of the traditions related to 1 Cor. 10:4; "Notes on Three Passages in St. Paul's Epistles," *The Expositor*, 3rd series, 9 (1889): 15–23. See also E. Earle Ellis, "A Note on 1 Corinthians 10:4," *Journal of Biblical Literature* 76 (1957): 53–56; reprinted in 1978 in his collection of essays entitled *Prophecy and Hermeneutic in Early Christianity* (Grand Rapids: Wm. B. Eerdmans Publishing Co., 1978), 209–212; G. B. Caird, "The Descent of Christ in Ephesians 4, 7–11," in *Studia Evangelica*, vol. 2, ed. F. L. Cross (Berlin: Akademie-Verlag, 1964), 535–545; Jan Willem Doeve, *Jewish Hermeneutics in the Synoptic Gospels and Acts* (Assen: Van Gorcum, 1954), 110–113; Henry St. John Thackeray, *The Relation of St. Paul to Contemporary Jewish Thought* (London: Macmillan & Co., 1900), 205–208.

5. See Doeve, *Jewish Hermeneutics*, 111.

6. *Tosefta Sukkah* (a rabbinic Jewish document, containing supplements to the Mishnah) 3:11. From Jacob Neusner, *The Tosephta*, 6 vols. (New York: KTAV Publishing House, 1977–1986), 2:220.

7. Compare Ex. 15:23–25 and *Tosefta Sukkah* 3:11–12. For a reconstruction of the "well" tradition, see Ellis, "A Note on 1 Corinthians 10:4," 53–54.

8. From *Midrash Rabbah: Translated into English with Notes, Glossary and Indices*, ed. H. Freedman and Maurice Simon (London: Soncino Press, 1939), vol. 5, p. 4.

9. Ellis, "A Note on 1 Corinthians 10:4," 53–54.

10. See the Midrash Rabbah on Num. 1:1, and compare the Lord's word to Moses in Num. 21:16 (". . . That is the well of which the LORD

said to Moses, 'Gather the people together, and I will give them water' ") with Num. 20:8.

11. See the reference to "Scribes" in Onkelos. *The Targum Onqelos to Numbers,* The Aramaic Bible, vol. 8, trans. Bernard Grossfeld (Wilmington, Del.: Michael Glazier, Inc., 1988), 126.

12. Philo, *Allegorical Interpretation* 2.86; *The Worse Attacks the Better* 115–119.

Epilogue

1. See Howard Clark Kee, *Knowing the Truth: A Sociological Approach to New Testament Interpretation* (Minneapolis: Fortress Press, 1989), 7–31.

2. Richard B. Hays, *Echoes of Scripture* (New Haven, Conn.: Yale University Press, 1989), 84–87.

For Further Reading

Beker, J. Christiaan. *Paul the Apostle: The Triumph of God in Life and Thought.* Philadelphia: Fortress Press, 1980.

Dunn, James D. G. *Christology in the Making: A New Testament Inquiry into the Origins of the Doctrine of the Incarnation.* Philadelphia: Westminster Press, 1980.

Ellis, E. Earle. *Paul's Use of the Old Testament.* Grand Rapids: Wm. B. Eerdmans Publishing Co., 1957.

Gager, John G. *The Origins of Anti-Semitism: Attitudes Toward Judaism in Pagan and Christian Antiquity.* New York: Oxford University Press, 1983.

Gaston, Lloyd. *Paul and the Torah.* Vancouver: University of British Columbia Press, 1987.

Hanson, Anthony Tyrrell. *Studies in Paul's Technique and Theology.* London: SPCK, 1974.

Hays, Richard B. *Echoes of Scripture in the Letters of Paul.* New Haven, Conn.: Yale University Press, 1989.

Hübner, Hans. *Law in Paul's Thought.* Trans. James C. G. Grieg. Edinburgh: T. & T. Clark, 1984.

Juel, Donald. *Messianic Exegesis: Christological Interpretation of the Old Testament in Early Christianity.* Philadelphia: Fortress Press, 1988.

Lindars, Barnabas. *New Testament Apologetic: The Doctrinal Significance of the Old Testament Quotations.* London: SCM Press, 1961.

McKim, Donald K., ed. *A Guide to Contemporary Hermeneutics: Major Trends in Biblical Interpretation.* Grand Rapids: Wm. B. Eerdmans Publishing Co., 1986.

Räisänen, Heikki. *Paul and the Law.* Philadelphia: Fortress Press, 1983.

Sanders, E. P. *Paul, the Law, and the Jewish People.* Philadelphia: Fortress Press, 1983.

———. *Paul and Palestinian Judaism: A Comparison of Patterns of Religion.* Philadelphia: Fortress Press, 1977.

Segal, Alan F. *Paul the Convert: The Apostolate and Apostasy of Saul the Pharisee.* New Haven, Conn.: Yale University Press, 1990.

———. *Rebecca's Children: Judaism and Christianity in the Roman World.* Cambridge, Mass.: Harvard University Press, 1986.

Siker, Jeffrey S. *Disinheriting the Jews: Abraham in Early Christian Controversy.* Louisville, Ky.: Westminster/John Knox Press, 1991.

Stendahl, Krister. *Paul Among Jews and Gentiles, and Other Essays.* Philadelphia: Fortress Press, 1976.

Thiselton, Anthony C. *The Two Horizons.* Grand Rapids: Wm. B. Eerdmans Publishing Co., 1980.

Westerholm, Stephen. *Israel's Law and the Church's Faith: Paul and His Recent Interpreters.* Grand Rapids: Wm. B. Eerdmans Publishing Co., 1988.

Index of Passages Cited